Post-communication

CRITICAL ANALYSIS AND EVALUATION

THE BOBBS-MERRILL SERIES IN *Speech Communication*

RUSSEL R. WINDES, *Editor*

ROBERT S. CATHCART

Post-communication

CRITICAL ANALYSIS AND EVALUATION

The Bobbs-Merrill Company, Inc.
INDIANAPOLIS AND NEW YORK

Copyright © 1966 by The Bobbs-Merrill Company, Inc.
Printed in the United States of America
Library of Congress Catalogue Card Number: 66-19701
ISBN 0-672-61073-6 (pbk)
Fifth Printing

Editor's foreword

A knowledge of the processes of criticism is essential even to an elementary understanding of speech communication. Most instructors of introductory speech courses fully realize this fact and organize their classes in such a way that much of their students' class time is spent in evaluating the speaking of their classmates. On a more advanced level, students are often asked to direct their efforts to reading and judging examples of public address.

Certainly, the beginning speech student can learn much simply by listening. It is our belief, however, that the student can make much more of his listening time if he is acquainted with a variety of theories about speech criticism. Without such background, he may unknowingly accept disorganized and superficial comments as genuine criticism. Without such background, his own critiques will probably lack the focus and rigor which mark informed judgments. Importantly, only with a basis for sound judgment may the student significantly improve his own communication and contribute to improvement in others.

We believe that Professor Cathcart's book on criticism will provide that fundamental knowledge by which a student can become a responsible critic. A reading of this volume should acquaint the student with a number of important principles and techniques. The book establishes a rationale for speech criticism based on the concept of choice. The basic assumption is that every communication is an attempt to exert control over others. Every speaker must choose the means whereby he will attempt to exercise influence. Through reference to rhetorical principles and insights from the behavioral sciences, Professor Cathcart provides the critic with a largely objective standard against which the speaker's choice of purposes, arguments, proofs, and style can be judged. In this connection, Professor Cathcart has reviewed the standards proposed by scholars for the evaluation of speech communication. Although he presents the Aristotelian "artistic" standard as a most useful system of criticism, he also introduces the systems of Burke and Richards.

In order to relate these concepts of criticism to the students' experiences, the book is organized in a progression of steps through which the student moves in appraising a speech. Thus, chapters move from analysis, through interpretation, to evaluations. To make these steps clearer, and more applicable, the more difficult concepts are illustrated with examples drawn from the literature of speech criticism.

Professor Cathcart treats criticism in its broadest context. He places the burden on the critic of judging not only the effects of speech, but their quality and social worth as well. In the final analysis, this volume, like the proper study of all criticism, is directed not so much at training either critics or performers, but at forming educated minds, capable of discipline and discrimination, and able to recognize the artistically and socially worthwhile.

Russel R. Windes

Contents

Acknowledgment, ix

1. **The nature of criticism**   *1*
    Speech as an object of criticism, 3
    The purpose of speech criticism, 6
    A rationale for speech criticism, 7
    Criticism and the student of speech, 11

2. **The methodology of criticism**   *14*
    Critical points of view, 15
    Standards for critical judgment, 20
    The tools of criticism, 26

3. **Analyzing the speech**   *32*
    Investigation and re-creation, 34
    The speech purpose, 39
    The rhetorical problem, 36

The lines of argument, 42
   The modes of proof, 45
   Organization, 52
   Style, 54
   Delivery, 58

4. Interpreting the speech — 60
   The speaker, 61
   The audience, 63
   The occasion, 69
   Non-Aristotelian interpretations, 73

5. Evaluating the speech — 89
   Problems of evaluation, 90
   The effects of the speech, 93
   The quality of the speech, 99
   The worth of the speech, 105
   Epilogue, 110

Bibliography, 112
Index, 120

ACKNOWLEDGMENT

I wish to express my appreciation to the many students and colleagues who have helped me in understanding speech criticism and the part it plays in the education of the student of speech. Particularly, I wish to acknowledge my indebtedness to Kenneth Hance, Lester Thonssen, Walter Fisher, Robert Kully, and Russel Windes, who have all contributed directly and indirectly to the development of this volume.

Post-communication

CRITICAL ANALYSIS AND EVALUATION

ONE
The nature of criticism

Communication is a word that describes the process of transferring meaning from one individual to another. Through the communication process, we interpret reality and select alternate paths of behavior. We employ communication so that we can exert control over the behavior of others. In speech communication, we seek to influence the attitudes and opinions of auditors in order to direct their behavior toward a predetermined goal.

That some communicators are more successful than others is apparent. But why some are more successful in controlling and directing behavior through speech, whereas others obtain only moderate success, or none at all, is not readily understood. It is often difficult to determine whether a particular message has been effective. Usually we know whether we like a speech, but being able to judge that speech as effective or influential is quite another matter. To evaluate the impact of a speech, one must know: (1) the purposes of the communicator; (2) the immediate and long-range effects of the communicative situation. If a speaker's goal is to win votes for his motion, and the motion passes after he has spoken about it, is one to conclude that his speech was influential? What of the speaker whose goal is to create a certain tolerance toward nonconformity on the part of his audience? How is his success to be judged? There is no vote—no motion to be passed. Contemporary methods of measuring attitude change might be useful in determining whether auditors were made more favorably disposed toward nonconformity by the communication. Yet the findings of these measurements could hardly be considered complete indicators of successful communication in a situation that involves imponderable attitudes, values, and opinions.

The problems of appraising a speech are extensive and difficult; however, such appraisal must be done. Necessity forces the speech critic into the frustrating but rewarding attempt to master the difficulties inherent in the art of criticism.

The speech critic engages in criticism so that he can determine the success of any given speech. If he is to judge certain speech communication effective and other communication ineffective, then he must evolve criteria by which he can discover communicative effectiveness. The formulation of criteria, as well as the application of the criteria to speech situations, are the tasks of the critic.

Criteria of critical appraisal are derived by the speech critic from his study of rhetoric, which has been defined as the philosophy and method of expressing thoughts, feelings, and motives through verbal and visual symbols for the purpose of behavioral control.[1] The critic measures the success of a speech by comparing it with a rhetorical ideal. Rhetorical theory encompasses an extensive body of literature, dating from ancient Greece to modern times, and includes pragmatic, empirical, and experimental studies of successful speaking. Through the study of rhetorical theory, the critic formulates theories and principles of good speech, principles that represent criteria for successful speaking.

The critic must approach the speech he is to criticize as objectively as possible. Unlike a member of an audience, he does not give a personal response to a speech. He does not say, "I like it," for, if he did, he would be making a statement of his own feelings and nothing more. Rather, he seeks to relate the communicative situation, including the message itself, to discovered principles of good speech. From such a relationship, he can make his evaluations and judgments about the quality of the examined speech. To be objective, the critic must view the speech from the perspective of both speaker and audience, so that he can make meaningful and

---

[1] For a thorough discussion of the scope of rhetoric, see Donald C. Bryant, "Rhetoric: Its Function and Scope," **The Quarterly Journal of Speech**, XXXIX (December 1953), 401–424.

incisive criticisms about the entire communicative event. Such a critique can help to make speakers better communicators and listeners more discriminating.

Despite the problems involved, criticism is a necessary activity. It is essential to the growth and success of all social activity and is particularly vital in humanistic studies. The humanist is concerned with arriving at formulations concerning the good in human endeavor, just as the scientist is concerned with arriving at formulations concerning the true in nature. The critic arrives at criteria or standards for what he believes to be excellence—whether that excellence be applied to art, music, drama, or speech. In so doing he plays a vital role. In all of the arts, the critic seeks the improvement of the art by reminding the art constantly of its potential. The critic insists that minimum standards be maintained; at the same time, he looks to innovations that will improve the quality of the art in the future. In the end, the critic hopes to play a significant role in the improvement of man himself. As Edwin Black phrased it, "Criticism is a discipline that, through investigation and appraisal of the activities and products of men, seeks as its end the understanding of man himself."[2]

The student of speech communication engages in rhetorical criticism. He attempts to assess the merit of purposive discourse. Like critics in other areas, he hopes through his criticism to improve the quality and effectiveness of speech communication and hence to improve man himself. In his work, he draws from the discipline of rhetorical criticism, but he is also a student of history, philosophy and ethics, and social-psychology. He studies any discipline that may aid him in his task of analyzing and evaluating human communication.

The basic purpose of this volume on criticism and evaluation is to assist in training knowledgeable, skilled, and responsible critics of speech communication.

Speech as an object of criticism

Speech rhetoric has long been considered the art of influencing the understanding, beliefs, attitudes, and conduct of others through

[2]Edwin Black, **Rhetorical Criticism** (New York: Macmillan, 1965), p. 9.

spoken language. It is common to man's everyday affairs and necessary to his functioning as a social animal. Aristotle began his **Rhetoric** by pointing out:

> ... all make some attempt to sift or to support theses, and to defend or attack persons. Most people do, of course, either quite at random, or else merely with a knack acquired from practice. Success in either way being possible, the random impulse and the acquired facility alike evince the feasibility of reducing the process to a method; for when the practiced and the spontaneous speaker gain their end, it is possible to investigate the cause of their success; and such an inquiry, we shall admit, performs the function of an art.[3]

Investigation into the successful performance of the art of discourse has led to that body of theory and method known as **rhetoric.** The formulation of rhetorical theory began in pre-Aristotelian times with the writings and teachings of the early Greek Sophists and the criticisms of Socrates, Thucydides, and Plato. Present knowledge of rhetorical principles has been derived from the study of past orators, rhetors, and critics. As men vied with each other in the ancient forums for places of leadership and sought to win support for their ideas in the Greek and Roman democracies, others studied and criticized their methods of speech, distilling them into works on effective discourse, such as Aristotle's **Rhetoric,** Cicero's **De Oratore** and Quintilian's **Institutio Oratoria.** Rhetors offered instruction in the art of discourse. From that time to the present, teachers and practitioners of rhetoric have been reformulating the principles and methods of effective speech based upon study of the most effective speeches of their times.

These principles are embodied in various treatises and textbooks, providing a philosophy of rhetoric and a means of practicing effective communication. From these theories and the best performance of the art come the criteria by which critics can assess communication and arrive at judgments of its effectiveness and worth.

As the study of speech-making reveals, speech is more than the application of a formula, more than a predictable scientific process; this is what makes it an object of criticism. Every speech is a creative effort to produce that arrangement of appropriate ingredients that will best serve the speaker's purposes. Because each

[3]Aristotle, **The Rhetoric,** trans. Lane Cooper (New York: Appleton, 1932), 1354a, 1.

speaking situation is different, the result of any speech is not completely determinable in advance. One cannot say that if a speaker performs steps **a, b,** and **c** he will achieve results **x, y,** and **z.** If this were possible, there would be no need for speech criticism. Only because speech is a creative, artistic endeavor is it an object of criticism. Only by examining a speech as it was composed and delivered to a particular audience on a specific occasion can the critic derive a judgment about its worthiness.

Because every speech involves an intricate relationship of the man and his ideas to the forms of language, to his hearers, and to his historical context, it is impossible for anyone to say what is the one right speech for any occasion. Both the speaker and the critic may perceive an ideal speech for that occasion, but only the performance of an actual speech will determine what is possible. The speaker must use his knowledge of the principles of effective communication to aid him in making the right choices for the achievement of that ideal speech. The critic must also use these same rhetorical principles to judge the speaker's choices and to determine how nearly the speaker achieved the ideal. In every case, the critic has before him a finished object that was created to accomplish certain ends. He can judge the strengths and weaknesses of the speech by applying rhetorical criteria learned from past speech-making, interpreting these principles in light of this particular endeavor.

We all know speech-making as a practical or utilitarian art. It is concerned with man's view of the world and his adjustment to it. A speech can be viewed as a purposeful and meaningful attempt on the part of the speaker to effect change, both in his hearers and in himself. If every communication has a purpose and therefore a goal, the critic can study and analyze it to ascertain how close it comes to achieving its desired effect and how suitable the speaker's intentions and means are to the circumstances that prompted the communication.

Purposiveness of speech provides one of the main justifications of criticism. Speeches do have effects on men's thoughts and actions, and the realization of a speaker's purpose could have important consequences for not only the immediate audience but for the whole community. Speeches do not have to be major in scope or purpose to produce effects; all speeches make their influence felt in the social sphere, and we must acknowledge the possibility that communicative intent has for the improvement or debasement of social thought and action. If speeches, even poorly constructed or ill-informed, can have consequential effects on listeners, then speeches must be studied just as any other phenomena that can influence the direction of social development. For man to have any control of his environment, he must be able to analyze those forces that influence him. Speech-making certainly falls in this category. Consequently, it is as much an object of study and criticism as other forms of art that influence man.

The purpose of speech criticism

"The basic justification for criticism of speaking is that here, as in other arts, criticism is both the way we tell ourselves what is going on and the way we learn how to practice the art with greater insight."[4] Mere participation in speech communication will not yield the understanding necessary to practice and evaluate the art more effectively. The trained critic is always needed, because those involved in the immediate communicative situation are seldom able to judge the communicative act unless they have been trained. The speaker is concerned primarily with whether he has gained the response he desired. The listener is concerned with discovering those things that will satisfy his own needs. Both speaker and listener tend to respond to the over-all impression the speech produces, not to its constituents. Both tend to be more concerned with the immediate rather than long-range effects. The speaker may be satisfied if he gained a sufficient amount of laughter and applause, and the listener—who laughed and applauded—may be dissatisfied because the speaker did not tell him anything new. Both may be entirely unaware of the rhetorical techniques that influenced their thinking, and unaware of what future effects could be produced by the speech. The trained critic, who may or may not be a member of the audience, performs a function different from that of the auditor-responder.

The critic, by removing himself from the speaker-audience relationship, and by assuming the role of analyst, seeks to determine what took place from both the speaker's and the listener's point of view. He analyzes the speaker's ideas, his arguments, his choice of

[4]John F. Wilson and Carroll D. Arnold, **Public Speaking as a Liberal Art** (Boston: Allyn and Bacon, 1964), p. 323.

language, his strategies, his vocal intonations—all the rhetorical devices the speaker has employed. Through this process, the critic fosters understanding of **the method of the speech** and knowledge of the way in which persons adapt their ideas to audiences and occasions.

The critic determines the response to the speech, both immediate and long range, and tries to account for this response. He asks: Was the speech effective? Did it fulfill its purpose? Did it achieve its intended goals? Then he attempts to determine what produced the response. By so doing, the critic reveals the operation of rhetorical theory in practice and clarifies understanding of that theory.

Beyond these matters, the critic looks at the whole communicative act to determine if it was significant and worthwhile. He asks: Were the speaker's intentions worthy? Did he tell the truth? Was he ethical in the means employed? Did his speaking serve to actualize the highest values of the society? The critic views speech-making as more than a set of technical skills, more than a nonmoral force to be appreciated no matter how base the goals of the practitioner. He evaluates the speech by applying standards of excellence garnered not only from the greatest speeches of the past but also from the highest aspirations of society. Criticism maintains the standards of rhetorical excellence.

Finally, only through responsible and intelligent criticism can we discover the limits of our present knowledge and seek new and better means of communication. The careful and thorough critic will find areas of human communication not adequately accounted for by existing rhetorical theory. He will discover where old theories no longer apply, and he will evolve new theory to account for unexplained matters. When rhetorical judgments cannot be made because knowledge and understanding are lacking or because new modes of communication are being developed, he will not try to bend his material to fit the old patterns of rhetoric, but will call for new explanations and new theories. The critic who helps us realize what we do not know about communication serves us well, and the critic who calls our attention to new or changing patterns of speech-making is a teacher as well as a critic.

A rationale for speech criticism

Each speaker has some purpose that prompts his communication. To accomplish his goal, he must of necessity employ rhetorical forms. He must present ideas, develop and support them, and organize them; he must use words and gestures; and he must employ vocal sounds and intonations. In each of these areas, he has a great variety of choice, and he has to select those means appropriate to his purpose. It is this **factor of choice** that makes each speech an individual creation, and it is this same factor that enables the critic to render a rhetorical judgment of the speaker's choices in relation to his purpose, the audience, and the occasion. Because the critic knows what choices other speakers have made, and because he also knows what is called for rhetorically, he can evaluate the choices in the particular speech under consideration.

This can be demonstrated through the hypothetical case of a Congressman who has been asked to address a local chamber of commerce audience about "foreign aid." Within certain limitations of subject and time, he has almost unlimited choice of the means by which he communicates his ideas to his audience. He may consider the nature of the audience and decide that the members would be most interested in learning about the amount of this aid, how it is distributed, and what its benefits are. As a result, he may choose to inform his audience about the way in which these programs are developed, paid for, and evaluated. On the other hand, he may look to his own beliefs and desires and decide that he wants to convince this audience that all foreign aid is undesirable and should be halted. Either way, he is forced to make choices about his goals. Whether he makes his choice after carefully weighing all the relevant factors—his own knowledge and beliefs, audience understanding and attitudes, the nature of the occasion—or simply plunges after the first idea that comes to mind, he has committed himself to a specific purpose or goal. **This commitment or choice can be objectively analyzed and reasonably evaluated by the critic.**

In the situation described, the critic, no matter what his personal beliefs, can examine the speaker's choice of purpose in terms of its appropriateness for the speaker, the subject matter, the audience, and the occasion. He can turn to the body of rhetorical theory pertaining to speech purpose and measure the speaker's choice against the relevant theory. He may find that the speaker misanalyzed the audience, that it was already well informed or even convinced that foreign aid should be abolished. Therefore, the speaker made a poor choice of purpose, trying to accomplish what had already been accomplished. The fact that the speaker may have pleased his listeners by saying things they already knew would make no difference in the critic's judgment of the inappropriateness of the speaker's purpose.

It is important at this point to remember that speeches do not just happen. They are put together, consciously or subconsciously, by speakers to fit a certain context. Speakers do not usually say the first things that come to mind. They select their words, guided by the circumstances in which they intend to speak and by their own needs. If the speaker is effective, it will be because he chooses words that are rhetorically appropriate to all the demands of the situation. Because there is always a matter of appropriate choice in light of these demands, the critic can say something **about** the speech as an effective communication.

A speech is not a matter of whim. If a person says things that are meaningless or inappropriate, he has not achieved communication. Such utterances cannot be criticized rhetorically. When, in normal communication, a person makes a statement, his listeners assume there is some reason for it and react accordingly. That the meaning of a remark may escape a listener does not change the fact that he assumes that some logical reason exists for what is said. The critic must also assume that every speaker had some definite communicative purpose that prompted him to make his statements. Given this assumption about the purposefulness of all speech, the critic can analyze a speech to determine that purpose, and he can then examine all other choices the speaker made in giving form and word to his purpose, judging whether or not these choices were rhetorically sound.

Without purposiveness, there would be nothing against which to judge a speaker's choices. If speech were a matter of whim or fancy, and results were unrelated to a goal, there would be absolutely no way of arriving at a judgment of the value or worthwhileness of a speaker's ideas and expression. If speakers did not care what resulted from their utterances, there would be no need for criticism and nothing to judge. It is precisely because speech is an instrument of adjustment and social control that it can be studied.

When a speaker himself is confused about what he wants, his listeners may believe that his speech has no purpose. He may have begun to talk before thinking through the situation carefully, without having formulated a set of goals. Nevertheless, the speaker expects to achieve something, or he would not have begun to talk. Maybe his purpose is to clarify his own thinking about the subject or perhaps to impress his listeners with his knowledge. That these are not worthwhile purposes and could result in negative reactions from the listeners does not change the fact that the speaker expects to accomplish something by means of his communication and is guided in his choice of words and ideas by this notion. Recognizing this, the critic can judge not only the effectiveness of choice of purpose, but also the effects of all the other choices made by the speaker.

Another matter that contributes to confusion about the dominant role of speech purpose is that the ostensible purpose of a speech may not be the real one. When a salesman says he is not trying to sell his product but merely wants to inform a prospective customer about the shortcomings of his competitor's product, his real purpose is to make a sale and not to impart information for information's sake. One usually judges such statements in light of what he knows the real purpose to be. It is more difficult to determine the speech purpose in those cases where speakers carefully disguise their intent. For example, a speaker may appear to be in favor of participation in the United Nations Organization, but in reality seek to "damn it with faint praise." The critic must carefully search all facets of the speaking situation to be sure he has found the speaker's purpose or purposes, because the evaluation of the speech will rest ultimately on the relationship between purpose and means employed.

By accepting this concept of speech as effective choice among a variety of alternatives, or as Aristotle called it, the "Faculty of discovering all the possible means of persuasion in any subject," the critic has a basis for comparison and judgment. He can compare the speaker's choices with those of other speakers and with the advice embodied in rhetorical theory. No matter what subject the speaker may pursue, the critic knows that the speaker must make choices about his purpose, arguments, proofs, language, and presentation. The critic can evaluate these choices and judge them for their rhetorical appropriateness to the speaker, the audience, and the occasion.

The critic's job is to determine whether the speaker discovered all the possible means of persuasion in the subject and also whether or not he made the most appropriate choices among them for that particular speech. For example, a speaker may be aware of the arguments in opposition to the proposal he is advocating, but choose not to mention them in hopes that the audience will think his plan is unopposed. It would be the critic's job to assess the appropriateness, rhetorically, of this kind of choice. Also, it would be the critic's function to evaluate the effect when a speaker failed to present a crucial argument because he was unaware of it. In all cases, the critic is looking at the rhetorical potential in the situation and measuring the speaker's choices against this.

Speeches do not just happen, and they cannot be strait-jacketed into one mold, for they are the unique result of the individual speaker's purposes, plans, and choices. Recognizing this, the critic who knows what would be ideal rhetorically can examine the choices the speaker made, analyze the results achieved, and make some defensible judgment about the appropriateness of the speaker's choices and the success of the speech.

Criticism and the student of speech

It is well established in educational theory that learning cannot take place without criticism. A person who wishes to learn a new task or to improve upon his performance of an old one, will not progress without some criticism. Simply doing something over and over will not necessarily result in improvement, unless the performance is analyzed and compared with a more ideal performance. If one does not know why he is failing to attain the results that he desires, he is not likely to improve. He must look at the task he is performing and be able to determine what is happening. Even knowing what is happening will not automatically lead to improvement, unless he has some awareness of the ideal performance. In each of these steps, criticism is involved. It may be self-criticism, or it may be the criticism of an instructor. Without it, no matter the source, there will be little learning.

Because of the important role of criticism in the learning process, it is essential that the student become a critic of speech if he hopes to improve his speaking ability. If he wants to communicate his ideas effectively, he must know the constituents of an effective speech. Moreover, he must know what happens to speakers and audiences in the process of communicating. He must study speakers and speeches and become familiar with their characteristics. He must know how they function and why they produce the effects they do.

The student bent upon improving his own speeches need not become a rhetorical scholar, but he must understand and use criticism, because there is no other road to improvement. Unless he learns for himself how to analyze and assess speech-making, he is likely to misunderstand criticism of his speeches by others. He would be unable to recognize and accept those assessments that are valid, while rejecting those that are specious. Furthermore, he would not develop the critical acumen that enables a person to become his own best critic.

Learning how to criticize speeches can be valuable to the student of speech beyond the area of self-improvement. As a student, he must study history. In any study of history, he will confront those statements that men have made in their attempts to resolve their problems and establish their institutions. The events of history are often the results of man's communication successes and failures, and the study of speeches given in those moments of great crisis can enhance a student's knowledge and appreciation of history. The speech critic has an advantage over others because he can use his special skills to understand why men spoke as they did, how their speeches reflected the ideas of the times, and how events were shaped by these ideas. Ernest J. Wrage has stressed this particular function of speech criticism:

> ... The very nature and character of ideas in transmission is dependent upon configurations of language. The interpretation of a speech calls for complete understanding of what goes into a speech, the purpose of the speech and the interplay of factors which comprise the public speaking situation, of nuances of meaning which emerge only from reading of a speech in the light of its setting. At this juncture a special kind of skill becomes useful, for the problem now relates directly to the craftsmanship of the rhetorician. The student who is sensitized to rhetoric, who is schooled in its principles and techniques, brings an interest, insight, discernment, and essential skill which are assets for scholarship in the history of ideas, as that history is portrayed in public speeches.[5]

[5]Ernest J. Wrage, "Public Address: A Study in Social and Intellectual History," **The Quarterly Journal of Speech,** XXXIII (December 1947), 456.

Besides being a practitioner of the art of speech and a student of history, the student is a member of a society that values persuasion above coercion. The success of such a society is dependent upon the ability of the general populace to discern among a myriad of communications, and to select, those statements that come closest to establishing the truths necessary for the successful functioning of the body politic. For this reason, every responsible citizen in our democracy must be a speech critic. As Thonssen and Baird point out:

> ... A semblance of order, a means of determining goodness and badness, a guide to action must be found if the pattern of talk is to be more than an indiscriminate gnarling of points of view. It is at this moment that the role of the critic takes on meaning. Criticism serves to bridge the gap between external stimulus and internal compulsion to belief and action.[6]

The study and criticism of speeches can be the full-time job of a professional scholar; it is also a necessary part-time job of every responsible citizen in a democratic society; and it is a vital part of the education of every student of speech.

[6] Lester Thonssen and A. Craig Baird, **Speech Criticism** (New York: Ronald, 1948), p. 4.

TWO

The methodology of criticism

Speech criticism has played a vital role in the development of rhetorical theory since Plato and Aristotle. Speech critics through their analysis and evaluation of speeches have contributed to our knowledge of rhetoric and to our understanding of the ways in which men grappled with problems and interpreted the world in the various stages of Western history. This is not to say that all speech criticism has been equally valuable, nor that all critics have agreed in their interpretations and judgments. Criticism has varied from period to period just as speech practice and pedagogy have varied. Instead of a uniform criticism with a clearly defined methodology, speech criticism has produced a variety of types and methods, depending on the critic and the prevailing social and political values.

Such variety still exists. A number of approaches can be taken, and critics may disagree about the proper end product of their criticism and on the best method of producing it. Should the critic adopt a method that evaluates the speaker's artistic skill, but that says nothing about the wisdom or truth of the speaker's counsel? Should his method focus on the effects of the speech on its immediate audience only, or should it reveal the whole historical and social setting and view the speech as a force in that milieu? The student must grapple with these and similar questions if he wishes to produce useful criticism of a process as complex and dynamic as speech.

This chapter will present briefly some of the traditional types of speech criticism and the methods and forms employed by critics. This will be followed by a consideration of four standards for critical judgment derived from the rhetorics of the past. The purpose will be to demonstrate the shortcomings of some of these approaches and standards and to suggest that certain others would be more useful and valuable to the modern speech critic. Finally, the section on the tools of criticism will discuss the steps to be followed by the critic as he proceeds with his task.

Critical points of view

Depending on their notions of the function and place of rhetoric in society, critics develop different methods for producing the form and content of speech criticism. These fall mainly into four types. One is primarily concerned with the man who made the speech. It focuses on the kind of man he was, what his ideas were, how he prepared and delivered his speeches, and what his influence was. Using this focus, the critic would, for example in a criticism of President John F. Kennedy's speeches, analyze Kennedy's New England family background, his schooling, his social outlook and value systems, the sources of his speech ideas, and his goals.

A second type of criticism concentrates on the speech as an end in itself. The speech is viewed in the same way that the literary critic views an essay or any other literary product. This type of criticism is concerned with stylistic and grammatical forms, the qualities of the language employed, the symbols used, and the universality of the appeals in the speech. The critic judges the speech by its qualities of beauty and permanence. Examples of this type can be found in the many criticisms of Ralph Waldo Emerson's "American Scholar Address," in which the literary merit of the speech is the central focus of the critic, and little attention is paid to the fact that it was prepared and delivered on the specific occasion of the Harvard annual Phi Beta Kappa address to a particular audience that the speaker wanted to influence.

A third type of criticism, referred to as **historical,** concentrates on an analysis and interpretation of the speech as a historical event. It is concerned with the forces that produced the occasion for the speech and influenced what the speaker said. Using this type, the critic analyzes the speech in a way similar to that of the historian who analyzes a battle, a revolution, an election, or the signing of a treaty and who tries to evaluate its historic importance. For example, a criticism of Andrew Jackson's "Bank Veto" message by this method would entail a study of the national bank movement, the economics of the times, the political pressures on Jackson, the various positions taken by legislators, and the other events that culminated in his decision to veto the bank legislation. Then the critic would evaluate the speech, examining how well it fit into its historical milieu and how effectively it controlled ensuing events.

The fourth type views the speech as a **persuasive form** designed to produce an effect on a specific audience at a given moment.[1] It concerns itself with a study of the audience and the occasion, the speaker's relationship to the audience, and with the speech itself as it was delivered, as well as the impact of the speech. This type of criticism approaches speech as a distinct form of discourse that can be interpreted adequately only when it is understood as a persuasive process that takes place at the moment the speaker is actively engaging his audience in an exchange of language and thought. Most contemporary speech critics use this type of criticism because it effectively utilizes the pertinent aspects of the other three types and yet makes an assessment based upon the unique qualities of the speaking situation. This type of criticism would analyze and interpret Emerson's or Jackson's statements as part of an interaction between speaker and audience. It would consider the speaker's purpose in speaking, his analysis of the audience and occasion, and the effectiveness of his adaptation of argument, emotion, language, and delivery to the subject, audience, and occasion.

It is the author's opinion that this fourth type of criticism is the most satisfactory because it is concerned with speech-making per se, with its unique forms and its place in human affairs. Only when the critic approaches speech as a persuasive process does he make a contribution to our understanding of communication that cannot be made by the biographer, man of letters, or historian.

Although the type of criticism that views speech as a persuasive

[1] For a detailed discussion of this type of criticism as contrasted to literary criticism see Herbert Wichelns, "The Literary Criticism of Oratory," in **The Rhetorical Idiom**, ed. Donald C. Bryant (Ithaca: Cornell University Press, 1958), pp. 5–42.

The methodology of criticism

form is widely used, there are different ways of carrying out this criticism. These differences usually stem from the critic's idea of the appropriate end product of his criticism. Does he seek to give the reader his own view of the speech, or a better understanding of the way in which the speech worked, or does he want to produce an appraisal of the effectiveness of its rhetorical devices? Thonssen and Baird name four different ways of criticizing: (1) impressionistic; (2) analytical; (3) synthetic; and (4) judicial.[2]

In **impressionistic** criticism, the critic gives his personal reactions to the speech, or speaker, or both. He points out what he agreed and disagreed with, what he liked and did not like about the speech as he viewed it. In **analytic** criticism, the critic concentrates on the speech itself and carefully analyzes it, pointing out structure, proofs, enthymemes, metaphors, alliterations, multisyllabled words, language patterns, and so forth. From this method, one gets something of an anatomical picture of the speech. In **synthetic** criticism, the critic goes beyond the speech itself, carefully reconstructing the entire speech occasion. He analyzes the setting and the audience; he describes what the speaker said and did; he recounts the audience reactions to the speech. In short, he faithfully **reproduces** the communicative act. In **judicial** criticism, the critic concerns himself mainly with judging the effectiveness of the speech. This type combines the elements of the other three ways of criticizing, but uses them only as a beginning point for interpretation and evaluation:

> . . . Thus, it [judicial criticism] reconstructs a speech situation with fidelity to fact; it examines this situation carefully in the light of the interaction of speaker, audience, subject, and occasion; it interprets the data with an eye to determining the **effect** of the speech; it formulates a judgment in the light of the philosophical-historical-logical constituents of the inquiry; and it appraises the entire event by assigning it comparative rank in the total enterprise of speaking.[3]

Only judicial criticism fulfills the functions of criticism described in the first chapter of this volume. Carefully describing a speech, labeling its constituents, and stating why the audience responded as it did are useful activities, but they do not constitute criticism. Only

---
[2] Thonssen and Baird, **Speech Criticism** p. 17.
[3] Ibid. p. 18.

by rendering reasoned judgments can the critic give us an understanding of the effectiveness of the speech rhetoric employed in a particular case and the value it might have for others who wish to communicate more effectively.

Adding to this variety of critical methodology, Edwin Black categorizes the approaches to speech criticism under three broad types of study. Depending on whether the critic uses a socio-political, a psychological, or a rhetorical approach to speech criticism, Black says there can be:

> (1) the movement study, in which the critic focuses on the total dispute over a single program or policy, from the genesis of persuasion on the issue to the time when public discussion of it finally ends; (2) the psychological study, in which the critic traces the patterns of influence between a rhetor's [speaker's] inner life and his rhetorical activities; and (3) the neo-Aristotelian study, in which the critic applies the rhetorical discourse canons derived from classical rhetoric, particularly the **Rhetoric** of Aristotle.[4]

Black finds the neo-Aristotelian approach the most widely used. In it, the critic begins with the Aristotelian definition of rhetoric as "the faculty of discovering in the particular case what are the available means of persuasion,"[5] and he uses the five canons (invention, arrangement, style, delivery, and memory) of rhetoric to analyze the speech and to determine how effectively the speaker utilized the available means of persuasion in adapting his ideas to the audience and occasion. He looks at each speech as a particular problem in persuasion between the speaker and the listener, in which the speaker must draw from the resources within himself, the subject, the audience, and the occasion to achieve his purpose, and to which the critic can apply the principles of effective discourse formulated by Aristotle and added to by his followers. Black believes that neo-Aristotelian critical studies are popular because the method is clear and easy to apply, and because it produces a criticism that is reasonably objective. He says:

> . . . By excluding the critic from the context of the discourse, . . . and by sanctioning only the sort of judgment that can be empirically verified; neo-Aristotelianism has provided a methodology that, inde-

---
[4]Edwin Black, **Rhetorical Criticism** (New York: Macmillan, 1965), p 18.
[5]Aristotle, **The Rhetoric,** trans. Lane Cooper (New York: Appleton, 1932), 1356a, 1.2.

pendently applied by different men to the same object, can yield the same conclusions.[6]

He warns, however, that there are at least two weaknesses and shortcomings in neo-Aristotelian criticism. It is rigid in form, and its methodology cannot always account for all the effects produced by a speech, particularly those rare displays of highly effective speech-making that seem to violate the traditional rules. Despite these weaknesses, most modern rhetoricians agree with the Aristotelian concept of speech as an art reducible to principles. These principles can be applied to any speaking situation to measure the performance and effect of the art.

Although this discussion has been concerned with different types and forms of criticism, the reader should realize that these differ less in substance and more in emphasis or focus. The critic who focuses on the speaker and the kind of man he was engages in a psychological study. Using certain Aristotelian canons, he might arrive at a judgment about the effectiveness of the man as a speaker. Another critic focusing on the speech itself and studying it as one in a series of speeches in the pre-Civil War Abolition Movement may be satisfied with analyzing the speech and nothing else, producing what Thonssen and Baird refer to as an "analytical criticism." There is over-lapping in these approaches to criticism, and often the critic can employ methods from each type in his assessment and evaluation of speeches. He needs to know the personality and background of the speaker; to place the speaker and the speech in their milieu; to study the ideas and arguments contained in the speech; and to study the effects of the speech on the audience and society. He ought to be able to analyze the speech and recreate the speaking situation, arriving at an empirically verifiable judgment. It is important that he not be satisfied with just one of these types of criticism, but that he seek that type of criticism or combination of types that will most satisfactorily reveal the speech and its impact.

To make an effective criticism of a speech is a challenging task, requiring use of all analytic skills and all methods that lead to an effective evaluation of speech-making. The rewards of such judicious criticism are great. It adds much to our knowledge and appreciation of good speech-making; it is one of the surest paths to increased effectiveness as a speaker; and, it can do much to improve

[6]Black, **Criticism**, p. 76.

the speech-making that is so important to the development of a free society.

Standards for critical judgment

The aim of criticism is to arrive at a judicious evaluation of a speaker's choices of content and form, compared with the principles of good rhetoric and an ideal performance. To accomplish this, standards must be developed by which to determine "the ideal" or "the most effective." To make statements about the validity of the speaker's arguments, or the effectiveness of his vocal inflections, criteria must be established for determining "good" or "best." Even if this is done on a comparative basis, i.e., by measuring one speech against a similar speech, the critic still has the problem of deciding which speech to use as the model. In short, he must have standards to begin with so that he can determine which speech is to be used as the one against which comparison will be made.

For centuries, rhetoricians and critics have addressed themselves to this problem of judging what is good, or best, or most effective. Plato made this his central concern, not only in rhetoric but in his whole philosophy. Discovering and perceiving the ideal in anything is essentially a philosophical problem. Without making deep philosophical investigations, however, it is possible to become familiar with some of the standards for judging speakers and speeches used by various critics in the past.

An examination of rhetorics of the past reveals that four general standards have been used to judge speeches. These are classified as: (1) the results standard; (2) the truth standard; (3) the ethical standard; and (4) the artistic standard. Each one has its proponents, and the following sections will briefly explore the advantages and disadvantages of each standard for arriving at a judicious appraisal of a speech.[7] The author believes that the **artistic standard** is the only one that can be used successfully in making judgments that can be verified by the application of Aristotelian methods. But first, what is entailed when the critic uses any one of these four standards of judgment?

The results standard. One standard for judging a speech is to

[7] For other discussions of the standards of judging speeches, see James H. McBurney and Ernest J. Wrage, **The Art of Good Speech** (Englewood Cliffs: Prentice-Hall, 1953), chapter II; and John F. Wilson and Carroll D. Arnold, **Public Speaking as a Liberal Art** (Boston: Allyn and Bacon, 1964), pp. 330–333.

judge it by its **results**. This standard works from the basis that, if the speaker accomplished his purpose, his speech was an effective or good one. Because speech is purposive, a means by which speakers attempt to bring about change or social control, then the speaker who effects a response in the desired direction, or the speaker who gains his end, must be judged as having given an effective speech. This standard for judging speeches, though simple in form, is not so easily applied as one might first think.

The critic who attempts to use **results** as his standard for judgment is immediately confronted with several problems. First, it is difficult to determine precisely what the results of a speech are. Does applause mean that the audience understood and accepted the speaker's ideas? Does the lack of overt response mean that the speech had no effect on the hearers? Is it possible to distinguish between temporary and permanent results? At what point do the effects of a speech end? Surely not at the close of the speaker's utterances. To take an example, Adolf Hitler spoke frequently to the German people, exhorting them to establish themselves as the master race of the world. Many were convinced by his words. Germany's actions resulted in World War II and death to millions of Germans, including Hitler. To what extent were these speeches responsible? Should they be judged by these long-term events or only by the results immediately following an individual speech? If one grants that the impact of Hitler's speeches go beyond the immediate response of the audience, how does the critic determine the ultimate combined results of Hitler's speeches?

Another problem confronting the critic who uses the results standard is that of determining whether or not the results observed are derived solely from the speech. Assuming that the response to a speech can be observed (for example, a situation in which a speaker makes a plea for an audience to donate money), the question of how much of the response is caused by the speech remains. Did all those who donated money do so as a direct result of the speech? Were those who did not donate unaffected by the speech? Many influences, operating before, during, and after a speech, determine human behavior. How can one separate these other influences from those of the speech? How can one judge the results of a speech if he cannot be sure which results were produced by the speech and which by other factors?

Recognizing that speech criticism should begin from the point that speech is purposive and that the speaker's choices of rhetorical devices are determined in the main by his intention to achieve results, it does not necessarily follow that the good speech is the one that gets results, or that getting results makes a speech a good one. As already pointed out, this standard cannot be applied realistically and meaningfully. Worse, its use can lead to situations in which the critic upholds as a good speech every fraudulent "sales pitch" that results in a sale, or condemns every speech that intentionally encourages men to live in peace and harmony with their fellow men.

The truth standard. A second and quite different standard for judging speeches is one that uses the criterion of **"truth."** According to this standard, if one cannot be certain of the results of a speech, he can determine the effectiveness of the speech by the degree to which it establishes or furthers the truth. The underlying assumption here is that ideally man should seek the truth as the best way of adjusting to both his environment and to his fellow man. Therefore, a speech that clarifies, upholds, or reveals truth is a good speech; any speech that falsifies ideas or misleads its hearers is bad or ineffective, no matter how well it succeeded in getting a favorable response.

Using the truth standard as the final measure of a speech is often attributed to Plato. He urged that the speaker be a philosopher who knew not only truth, but understood the nature of the soul. The ideal speaker is therefore concerned with making truth prevail among men rather than persuading audiences to his own ends.

Plato's idea of the use of truth as the measure of all things is extremely appealing to philosophers and critics alike. Most of us seek accurate facts, honest reasoning, correct answers, and the "right" course in everyday affairs. We realize that decisions are no sounder than the truth that went into their making, and we usually deplore speakers who distort facts and mislead us with their reasoning when the outcome is very important to us. This desire to eliminate the false and establish the true, however, does not necessarily make truth the only measure of the effectiveness of a speech.

As with the results standard, it is not easy to determine what truth is. Most speech-making arises from controversy and deals with those things in life that are contingent and probable, i.e., speeches are created by those very situations in which men are in doubt about the truth or the right course of action. If everyone was in agreement on what was true and what needed to be done, there would be no need to make speeches. It is when they are in doubt, when they are faced with problems (Should Communists be allowed to speak on our campuses? Are Negroes justified in their civil rights demonstrations?) that men are prompted to speak, to debate, to exhort. That there is so much speech-making about such problems is an indication that we do not yet know where the truth lies.

If there are many areas where the truth is unknown, then the critic is not going to be able to use truth as the standard for his judgment. The critic is not omniscient; he does not have a handy pocketful of truth by which to measure speeches. Even if he waits until a speech has been tested by time and experience, he will not necessarily find that final truth by which he can judge. More than twenty-five hundred years ago, Socrates said:

> ... if the soul exists before birth, and in coming to life and being born can be born only from death and dying, must she not after death continue to exist, since she has to be born again?[8]

What is "the truth" by which to judge this argument?

The second problem with using the truth as the only standard for judging a speech is that it can force a critic to rank a speech as a good one when the speaker knows the truth, even though he presents it in such a disorganized manner that he thoroughly confused his hearers. In this case, though the speaker spoke the truth, he may actually have set back the cause of truth. Using the truth standard, the critic would have to judge the speech as good. Just as speakers falsify evidence and advocate illogical positions to cover untruths, so can speakers confuse and confound audiences about the truth. Both kinds of speaking should be condemned, philosophically and rhetorically.

The ethical standard. If a speech cannot be judged by truth alone, some critics say that it should be judged by **the speaker and his motives,** i.e., by applying an **ethics** standard. If the speaker is an honest and truthful man and desires to uphold that which is good and noble, will he not speak the truth and attempt to persuade people to that which is good? This theory makes the personality,

---

[8]Plato, "Phaedo," **Plato Selections**, ed. Raphael Demos (New York: Scribner's, 1927), p. 177.

the character, and the motivations of the speaker the standard by which to judge speeches. The "Good Man Theory," often attributed to Quintilian because of his statement, "that no man, unless he be good, can ever be an orator,"[9] is based on the assumption that good men will speak effectively because they **are** good. That is, their understanding and knowledge of what is right and wrong will lead them to employ only the most desirable methods of persuasion, and always with good intentions.

This is similar to Plato's truth standard—an attempt to set up a standard that will condemn those who use rhetoric for wrong ends and praise those who seek to lead men to more noble ends. The ethical or good man standard of judgment has the same weaknesses as the truth standard. One cannot always determine which speaker is the good man. Often, a speaker's motives are not clear until long after the speech; they are frequently a mixture of both selfish and lofty aims. Sometimes a speaker with the best of intentions will mislead an audience or advocate an incorrect course of action. Not only is it improbable that one can know for certain that a man is a good man; if this is accepted as the sole standard, the critic would be forced to adopt the position that a good man could not give a bad speech. Certainly, this latter position could not withstand a pragmatic test.

The results theory, the truth theory, and the ethical theory all have one common denominator: they look **outside** the speech itself to find some measure that can be used to judge the speech. The results standard looks to the audience response, the truth standard to the righteousness of the speaker's goal, and the ethical standard to the worth of the speaker's intentions. Granted that all of these are important considerations in every speech, they are not the fundamental considerations. The art of speech is concerned with the ways in which men use language and thought to give effectiveness to truth, to portray their good intentions, and to move audiences to the desired responses.

The artistic standard. In judging a speech, the critic's standard should be the **artistic worth** of the speech, or how well the speaker utilized the principles of effective speech-making. The **artistic standard** of judgment is based on the assumption that there are principles of rhetoric (derived from the study of the best speeches

[9]Quintilian, **Institutio Oratoria,** trans. John S. Watson (London: Heinemann, 1891) II. 392.

of the past) to guide our efforts to communicate, and that these principles can be employed effectively or ineffectively, depending on our understanding of them. These rhetorical principles take into account that truth is more persuasive than falsehood, that a man of good character is more likely to be believed by his hearers, and that responses that are in keeping with the noble aims of man are likely to be more readily achieved and longer lasting. This standard considers the forms and methods by which a speaker demonstrates these things to an audience, and measures a speech by how well or artistically the speaker employed the available means of persuasion on a given speech occasion.

When the critic uses the artistic standard as his measure of speech effectiveness, he does not ignore results, truth, or the ethics of the speaker. He studies audience response insofar as he can determine it, and he attempts to account for that response. More importantly, he determines as best he can the responses the speaker sought and analyzes the methods used to achieve them, judging whether or not the means are commensurate with the desired responses. The critic may not be sure what the results of the speech will be, but he can judge how close the speaker will come to achieving desired results given the rhetorical methods employed. The critic using this standard will always condemn those things in a speech that are obviously untrue. He will evaluate arguments for insufficient or incredible data, for errors and fallacies in reasoning, and for improper motivational appeals, because they falsify truth. The critic will not judge truth as an absolute but will judge how near the speaker came to establishing or revealing truth.

The same holds true for the speaker's ethics. The critic will analyze and judge the means by which the speaker reveals his sincerity, his trustworthiness, and his knowledge in the speech. The critic will not make absolute judgments about the speaker as a man, but will judge the man as a speaker. He will condemn the speaker who misleads an audience about his expertness or authority. He will equally condemn the speaker who is an authority but fails to reveal this to his listeners thus depriving them of one of the means they have of determining the appropriate response to the speech.

The artistic standard for speech criticism sets as its goal the ideal performance of the art, as that ideal has been derived from the study of those speeches that have stood the test of time and have been universally acclaimed for their excellence. It attempts to ascertain the highest achievement possible in any speech situation and then uses that as the measure of a particular speech. This requires the critic to know rhetorical theory, to understand the speech process, to analyze its constituents, to determine its potential, and judge its effect.

The tools of criticism

Thus far, discussion has concerned the ideal type of speech criticism—judicial criticism of a speech as a purposeful act involving a speaker, a subject, an audience, and an occasion. It has considered the ideal standard to be applied in making a judgment: the artistic worth of the speech. Now let us consider **how** to judge the artistic merits of a speech.

A speech is an extremely complex phenomenon, and so the process of investigation is not simple. A speech is more than the text on the printed page; it is more than can be heard by any one person; it is more than a series of words and statements; it is more than a process of sending and receiving sound waves. Consequently, the evaluation of a speech must be carried on at several levels. If this caveat is not adhered to, then the application of standards and the arriving at a judgment will be seriously impaired.

The critic can best grapple with these complexities if he employs a procedure that will insure that he has a firm grasp of the speech **before** he makes value judgments. This is most readily accomplished when he follows the four-step procedure of (1) **description:** understanding what went on in the speech; (2) **analysis:** considering why it went on; (3) **interpretation:** determining the meaning and effect of the rhetorical methods employed; and (4) **evaluation:** judging the quality and worth of the speech. The first two steps are essentially investigatory. The critic is concerned with the materials of the speech and with the way in which they are put together. The final two steps are judgmental. The critic combines his knowledge of rhetoric and his standards of judgment with what he has learned from his investigation and makes inferences or judgments. The remainder of this chapter will be devoted to a discussion of these four steps.

Description. The competent critic must be a careful observer, and he must **know what** to observe. By bringing his knowledge of speech-making to bear, he sees and hears things in the speech that others might overlook, just as the medical doctor does when he examines a patient. The layman may see only that the person "looks" sick, but the doctor observes the color of the skin, the dilation of the pupils of the eye, the pulse rate, the reflexes, and so on because he knows what to look for. The average listener hears only the speaker's words and sees his manner of presentation. The critic is aware of the speaker's purpose, his pattern of organization, his lines of argument, his modes of proof, his attitude toward the subject and the audience, and so forth. The critic observes carefully to catch the nuances of language and thought, to detect strategies, to ferret out the implied premises. In this step, the critic **describes** these things along with what he has observed about the setting, the audience, its reactions, and the speaker. In other words, **he reveals the speech** insofar as his understanding and grasp of what took place will permit.

Analysis. Comprehending the speech goes beyond mere description no matter how complete it may be. Describing what took place in a communicative act will avail little if one does not also understand **why** it took place. The **why** of a speech demands that the critic **analyze** what he has described. This step requires the critic to inquire into the speaker's choices (and their alternatives) and his execution of them, in order to grasp how the speaker perceived the situation and why he employed the principles of rhetoric as he did. The critic seeks to determine what the speaker had in mind when, for example, he began his speech with a personal anecdote, used fear-arousing appeals, or used a rapid rate of delivery. In other words, the critic attempts to ascertain why, rhetorically, the speaker did what he did. This analysis is not confined to the finished speech alone, but analyzes the speech as a process involving a time, place, audience, and idea. When the critic has completed this step, he should not only have a grasp of the speech but an understanding of why it functioned as it did.

An accurate description and analysis of a speech will put the critic "in possession" of the speech. He is now ready for the final two steps in this procedure: those of applying the principles and standards of rhetoric to the speech act in order to interpret and judge it. In this second phase, the critic makes judgments by **inter-**

preting and evaluating what he found through his investigation and analysis.

Only after the critic has studied the whole speech act from a rhetorical point of view, understanding as best he can what took place and why, is he in a position to make judgments. To make judgments that are meaningful and justifiable, he must **interpret** and **evaluate** the rhetorical constituents he has discovered in the speech. He must ascertain the effects of these constituents, including in his opinion what could be achieved, and how close the speaker came to succeeding in an artistic sense.

Interpretation. The **interpretive** step in criticism is a critical one in that it helps the critic to understand what judgments should be made. This step bridges the gap between the **how** and **why** of the speaker's rhetorical choices and performance and the **meaning** of these choices in terms of their rhetorical worth. Determining that a speaker has employed some rhetorical technique and with good reason is not basis enough for judging its worth. It is necessary to assess its meaning and effect for that particular speech on that specific occasion. A speech may contain recognized rhetorical devices, but they may not be effective in that particular instance. For example, it is recognized that simile can be effective in making ideas clear and vivid. President Kennedy, in his Inaugural Address, used the simile, "those who ride the tiger's back may end up inside." He used this simile to warn newly arising nations of the dangers of accepting Soviet aid to achieve their national goals. It is not enough for the critic to be aware of this simile and its reason for inclusion in the speech. He must consider rhetorically what effect it had and what it is worth. He must ask, how appropriate is this simile to the purposes of the speaker, how suited to the needs of the audience, how sound is it, how appropriate is it to the idea being furthered? And, he must answer these questions, in order to interpret the **meaning** of what has taken place.

Evaluation. Once the critic has interpreted the rhetorical constituents of a speech, he is in a position to **evaluate** these and make his judgment of their worth. To do this, the critic must have some concept of the ideal speech; he must understand what resources are available in the speaker, subject, audience, and occasion and what constitutes appropriate, skillful, and responsible use of them. This is the ultimate aim of the critic—to make a decision, to deliver a judgment. He has to appraise the strengths and weaknesses of the speech by evaluating all the important aspects of it and by judging whether they were artistically performed, whether effective or ineffective, and whether they contributed to truth or not.

At this point, the critic's own attitudes and values play a decisive role. Every critic must choose among the many factors operating in the speech and select those most significant for an assessment of the speech. This selection of significant factors involves his own value system as he determines what is important and what is unimportant. The critic must again apply his values as he reaches a final decision about the worth of each of these constituents. The best critical judgment, then, is the one that is undergirded by a firm understanding of speech-making and a well-conceived system of values for relating speech-making to that which is most worthwhile in human endeavor.

Each of us, no doubt, carries with him certain absolutes for judging truth, ethical conduct, and justice; and these all come into play when we judge anything, including speech-making. These absolutes alone are not enough in making a defensible critical appraisal of a speech. The critic needs to know something about how speeches in the past have been judged and what has been learned from these past performances and the judgments made of them. He needs some standards of comparison to aid him in making and justifying his judgments. He should study model speeches of all types to learn how men have achieved desirable results on other occasions and how their efforts have been judged. In this way, he can develop a standard of comparison for use in making evaluative judgments.

Naturally, the student of communication will have a greater store of knowledge and understanding to draw upon when he makes judgments than will the layman. But even the layman has had numerous experiences with speech-making and has his own set of models to which he compares the speech he is hearing. To the degree that he understands all the constituents of these model speeches and how they function rhetorically, he is able to arrive at a more learned or valid judgment of the speech at hand. If, for example, he knows something about the rules of evidence, he may be able to make a very accurate appraisal of the evidence in the speech; but if he knows nothing about the ways in which emotional proofs are developed and presented, he will be unable to make a meaningful judgment of this constituent of the speech. This is why an expert's critical judgment is more likely to be valid than that of a nonexpert; he knows what to look for and what to compare it with.

This does not mean that trained critics will all arrive at the same judgment of a speech—any more than drama critics and art critics always agree. Criticism is as much an art as is speech-making, and, as such, it is a highly individual affair. Each critic must analyze and evaluate a speech as **he** perceives it and as **he** understands what constitutes effective speech-making. This does not imply that there are no agreed-upon standards and that the field is wide open to any kind of an appraisal. More than twenty-five hundred years of speech-making and a considerable body of criticism can be drawn upon, as well as the study of criticism itself. From these areas have come the recognized, and, for the most part, accepted, principles of rhetoric and methods of criticism. However, each critic must learn these things for himself and apply them as he understands them. Each time he makes a criticism, he is adding something of his own to this body of knowledge.

When critics have arrived at different judgments of a speech, the **case** that the critic makes for his judgment can be examined. The critic who presents the **more complete** criticism, showing that he has understood more of what went on in the speech than another critic, may be considered as having given the better criticism. Or, the critic who presents sound support for his judgments may be considered a better critic than the one who delivers judgments but cannot demonstrate how he arrived at them. In each situation, one has not only the critic's final evaluation of the speech but all the description, analysis, and interpretation that supports this judgment. The critic who presents the best case in support of his judgments can be considered the better critic for the moment.

Each critic must **assume the burden of proof** for his interpretations and evaluations. In other words, he cannot expect that his judgments will be accepted simply because he is playing the role of critic. Each time he makes an assertion about a speech he has to support it. He is subject to the same rules of analysis, evidence, and reasoning that any commentator is. He must convince his hearers or readers that his criticism is valid.

Here is the final function of the critical method; the criticism must finally be communicated to a reader or hearer. It must be so communicated that the critic's analysis is clear, his interpretation meaningful, and his evaluation valid. In the end, criticism itself must meet the standards of good communication.

THREE

Analyzing the speech

The speech critic faces several problems unique to the art of speech. A speech is designed for a particular audience at a specific time and place. Once it has been presented, it has completed its function and never exists in that exact form and condition again. To grasp the full import of a speech, the critic must view it as a dynamic interaction between speaker and audience. One can examine a piece of sculpture as a critical object, giving little consideration to when it was created and who first saw it; not so with a speech. It can never be studied as existing apart from the dynamic relationships that produced it and that give it meaning.

To criticize a speech successfully, one must **possess it as a speech,** not as a printed manuscript apart from the setting. Ideally, the critic should be present when the speech is given, so that he can both see and "feel" what is happening. When he is present, he can observe the speaker and the audience; he can catch the mood and tone of the occasion; he can sense the moments of tension and empathy; he can relate all this to what is being communicated. Yet, even in this supposedly ideal situation, it is not easy to "hear" all of a speech and to retain the ideas and words for purposes of analysis. If the critic is listening closely for proof, he may be unable to observe the speaker's use of style or organization. If he is trying to evaluate audience reaction, he may ignore a key argument in the speech. The critic has many functions to perform, but he is limited in the amount of material he can perceive and retain while performing necessary critical tasks.

To function most effectively, the critic should have an advance copy of the speech to follow while he hears it. Careful study of the text is necessary in order to grasp the organization of a speech, to see how the speaker's thoughts unfold, and to understand the modes of proof. Even though the listening audience may not be conscious of all of these factors, they have an influence upon audience response, nonetheless, and it is the job of the critic to account for all possible effects of the speech.

Further complicating the critic's understanding of a speech in its entirety is the fact that it may have more than one audience. Often speeches are carried in the newspapers and are reproduced in part or as a whole on radio and television. When this is true, the speech has both an immediate audience (the one physically present), and a removed audience (a regional, national, or international audience that receives the speech via the mass media). Both are part of the total audience. **Removed audiences must be considered as part of the speech situation, because the speech affects them and they, in turn, affect what the speaker chooses to say.** The critic may find the speech has been altered to fit these various audiences. For example, when President Dwight D. Eisenhower spoke at Oklahoma City in 1957 on the measures taken to offset the gains made by the Russians when they launched the first earth satellite, he had an immediate audience of ten thousand persons, a radio and television audience of approximately thirty million, and a large national and international audience that read the speech in the newspaper. The speech seen and heard by the immediate audience and the network audiences had a rather lengthy introduction, in which the President commented on his past experiences in Oklahoma, acknowledged the University of Oklahoma championship football team, and made references to the grandson he had with him. None of these remarks was carried in the newspaper version of the speech, but they undoubtedly affected the image of the speaker for the audiences that heard them. In this case, the critic would have to know of both versions of the speech and be aware of the diverse audiences to understand what took place and why.

Investigation and re-creation

An accurate speech manuscript, or, preferably, a tape or video recording of the speech, will best serve the critic. If he does not have these aids, he must rely upon his ability to take notes, to recall, and to learn from others what was said. To say the least, it would be embarrassing for a critic to claim that the speaker failed to present evidence in support of a premise when the speaker actually did present it. This sort of lapse would invalidate the judgments of the critic pertaining to this aspect of the speech, if not the whole speech.

Usually, the critic is not present at the time a speech is delivered. He has to make a careful investigation to determine what was said, what the setting was, and how the audience responded. To do this, the critic may use newspaper and magazine accounts; he may use interviews of those present during the speech; he may question the speaker about his purposes, his preparation, and his reactions while giving the speech. The critic may also use historical and biographical data to further his knowledge of the speech setting. That the critic may not be able to obtain information from all these sources does not obviate the need to establish, as accurately and completely as possible, what took place in the speech act. Only to the degree that the critic can faithfully recreate the speech, can he make an accurate analysis of it.

Depending on where and when the speech was given, the amount of data the critic can accumulate may vary considerably. The older a speech is, the more difficult it is to recreate. The more obscure the occasion or the speaker, the more difficult it is to locate detailed accounts. At the very least, the critic who would study a past speech needs a reasonably accurate manuscript of the speech plus some basic information about the nature of the audience and the type of occasion. To the degree that his data is limited, his analysis will be partial and his judgments tentative. (The burden of establishing the authenticity of the text and the data he is using falls upon the critic.)

A word should be said concerning the authenticity of speech texts. The best copy of a speech would be a motion picture or a video tape with a sound track. This would be as faithful a reproduction of the total speech as one could hope to obtain. Next best would be a tape recording of the voice of the speaker, including the reactions of the audience as the speech was presented. Unfortunately, such electronic reproductions of speeches are rare. More frequently, the critic will have to rely upon printed copies of the speech, and sometimes these are inaccurate or incomplete.

There are only three sources of speech copy: the speaker himself, stenographic notes, or copies from a voice recording. In the latter two cases, copying errors or misinterpretations are almost always made. Although such errors are usually minor, serious changes or omissions could occur. If the copy of the speech comes from the speaker, then it is usually a prespeech release, or it is produced by the speaker sometime after the speech. Prespeech releases need to be checked for two common omissions. One is the omission of introductory statements directed to an immediate audience. This happens when the speaker ad libs his opening remarks or fails to write them out until the last moment; or he may prepare one introduction for his immediate audience and a different one for the press audience, as in the Eisenhower Oklahoma speech. A second type of omission in prespeech manuscripts involves the "off-the-cuff" remarks, interpolations, additions, deletions, and other alterations of the speech made during its actual presentation. Adlai E. Stevenson, for instance, in his 1952 and 1956 Presidential campaigns frequently added humorous remarks to his speeches that did not appear in the prespeech press releases. Frequently, such adaptations to the audience and occasion are significant.

When a manuscript is written by the speaker **after** the speech, it presents other problems. If the speaker has written from recall, there may be a great discrepancy between what the audience actually heard and what the speaker thinks he might have said. If the speaker has drafted a new copy of the speech from an original or rough manuscript, he may have yielded to the temptation to "spruce it up" so that it reads well. There is the famous case of Senator Borah's summary speech for the prosecution in the **Haywood v. Idaho** trial in 1907. When asked by newsmen for copies of this speech, Borah rewrote the conclusion, adding three paragraphs. The revised version became widely accepted as the actual speech. Ironically, the most frequently cited excerpts from this famous speech are taken from the three paragraphs that were never heard by the jury![1] Similarly, "official" documents such as the **Congres-**

[1] David H. Grover, **Debaters and Dynamiters** (Corvallis: Oregon State University Press, 1964), pp. 250–251.

sional Record carry corrected versions of the speeches made on the floor of Congress, as well as additional remarks and "speeches" that were never actually delivered, but only added to the **Record.**

The critic cannot naively assume that the copy of a speech he first happens across is an authentic or complete one. He must consider the possibility of error in transcribing speech, the frequent alterations and omissions in speech manuscripts, and the tendency of newspaper, magazine, and book editors to rewrite and reform speeches that they print. He must often play detective and piece together the best possible manuscript. If he is not sure of its accuracy, he must say so and limit his analysis and evaluation accordingly.

The same caution holds true for information about other aspects of the speaking situation. The critic must ferret out all he can about the audience and setting and make the best case based on the evidence available to him. Only by coming as close as possible to recreating the communicative act can he be assured that he has a sound basis for his analysis of the speech.

The rhetorical problem

One of the most useful approaches to speech analysis is to look upon a speech as a problem-solving process. A speaker has a problem to solve. He wants something from the audience, he wishes to attain a goal. Obstacles stand in the way of that goal, and the speaker can follow alternative paths to overcome these. For example, a speaker wishes to convince his hearers that capital punishment is an evil and should be abolished. His goal is to gain their assent to this belief. Some of the obstacles that stand in his way are: (1) many of his hearers have long accepted, without question, that capital punishment is desirable; (2) many of them are apathetic; (3) they do not consider the speaker an expert or particularly well-qualified in this field; (4) they have very little factual information about, or first-hand knowledge of, capital punishment; (5) many hold attitudes of vengeance and fear concerning criminals and would like to see more of them put to death as a way of stopping crime. In addition to these particular obstacles, the speaker faces the normal obstacles present in the communicative situation: language usage and meaning, hearing and understanding, physical and mental distractions, and lack of interest. How to surmount these obstacles and achieve the desired goal is the speaker's **rhetorical problem.**

If the critic approaches a speech by asking how the speaker perceives of and resolves his rhetorical problem, he will find that he has a better basis from which to develop an analysis of the speech. Instead of examining the introduction of a speech, for example, to see which of the recommended rhetorical devices the speaker used to gain attention and focus interest, the critic should consider what kind of a problem the speaker faced in introducing his speech and how he went about solving it. Was the situation one in which the audience was hostile toward the speaker because of prior knowledge of his ideas and activities, or perhaps because it had just listened to two long and boring speeches and did not want to hear another speaker? Given such a problem, the critic can ask, "Did the speaker perceive it as such? If not, why not? And, if so, what did he choose to do about it?"

Proceeding in this manner, the critic has something on which to base his analysis throughout the speech. If, for example, the speaker relies heavily on statistical data in his speech, the critic can look for the problem that made the speaker choose the use of statistics. Did he think that his audience was one that relied heavily on numerical data in reaching its conclusions, or did he think it lacked faith in his knowledge and therefore would be impressed if he could demonstrate that he had specific knowledge through his use of numerical data? In this way, the critic can say **why** the speaker used the rhetorical devices he employed instead of merely identifying and labeling them.

Locating and describing the speaker's rhetorical problem makes for a realistic approach to the analysis of a speech. It embraces the idea of speech as **purposeful** behavior and recognizes that the speaker is exercising **choice** as he attempts to accommodate his ideas and desires to the persuasive demands of the subject, audience, and occasion. Human beings believe and behave as they do because it satisfies their needs, and they will not change simply because a speaker wants them to. Therefore, whether a speaker knows it or not, he has a problem each time he sets out to alter beliefs and behavior by means of oral discourse. The critic must see and understand the rhetorical problem that is the beginning point of every communication.

Eugene Vasilew illustrates the significance of this understanding. In his criticism of a speech by Norman Thomas, American Socialist party head, and six times its candidate for President, to the Townsend Convention of August 1936, he described the particular rhetorical problem:

> This speech to the Townsend Convention was at least the third time Thomas had chosen Townsendism as a theme for a major address, but is was the first time he spoke directly to Townsendites. . . . his stand in opposition to the Plan was more or less public knowledge.
>
> Many of the Townsend partisans at the convention must have been aware of Thomas' sentiments about Townsendism; others knew him only as a socialist and, as this term was loosely interpreted, it could easily have meant "muscovite agent" to them. . . .
>
> For Thomas, the invitation to address the Townsend Convention was a signal opportunity. Not only did he have a captive audience composed of people who were hearing him for the first time in this campaign, it was also a bigger audience than he could normally expect to get.
>
> As a presidential candidate, his ostensible purpose in addressing the convention was to win votes for his candidacy. But he eschewed this purpose for what he believed to be a more important duty; to destroy the economic illusion that Townsendism had created. He sought to persuade the Townsendites to relinquish their struggle for the Plan and to turn their energies in more useful directions, that is, towards the achievement of socialism.
>
> . . . Given an opportunity to address directly the leaders and many followers of the movement, Thomas attempted a miracle in speech-making. It was as if he came to the Democratic national convention in the hope of nominating a staunch Republican.
>
> It was, in fact, even more difficult than that. He was asking an assembly, which for three days had had its solidarity cemented and confirmed, to disown its very reason for existence. Even more, he was asking these blind adherents of Townsendism to relinquish their faith and give up their hope.
>
> It is perfectly clear from the speech itself that he knew what he was doing and that he deliberately chose to sacrifice votes and perhaps a greater personal triumph in order to put himself on record. He made this point in his peroration:
>
> "You don't suppose I stand up here and talk with you frankly because it is fun; do you think I don't know how to make speeches you would applaud? I would not have to tell you that I didn't agree with

you in every respect. I could make a speech about liberty, about freedom, about abundance, about 'down with the bankers'—I could make them, and they would be true, but I want to talk seriously with you. . . ."

Having decided on this course, what then was his rhetorical problem? It may be stated in five parts as follows:

1. To exercise tremendous personal appeal. The initial suspicion, if not antagonism, of the audience would have to be allayed.
2. To appeal to stronger motives than those which had already led the audience to accept Townsendism.
3. To offer an alternative which would satisfy the same wants as Townsendism, and to make the alternative palatable.
4. To make his entire approach emotional. It should have been apparent to him that the audience was in no mood to listen to carefully developed logical arguments.
5. At almost any cost, to keep from making the audience more negative or antagonistic to himself or his ideas.[2]

The speech purpose

The critic, in determining the speaker's rhetorical problem, must give consideration also to the speaker's purpose or intent. It is obvious in the Vasilew analysis of Thomas' speech that one cannot discuss the rhetorical problem without knowing the speaker's purpose, and vice versa. Because purpose is central to all discourse, it plays an important part in both analysis and evaluation of speech. For the same reasons, the critic cannot evaluate the effect of rhetorical devices on the audience without knowing what response the speaker was seeking.

One method of analyzing speech purpose used by critics both ancient and modern is to divide all speech-making into general categories, based either on the setting for the speech or on the mental response sought by the speaker, e.g., deliberative speeches, courtroom speeches, and ceremonial speeches; or speeches of understanding, speeches of conviction, speeches of stimulation, and so forth.[3] Using such an approach, the critic determines in which category the speech rightly belongs and thereby defines its general

---

[2] Eugene Vasilew, "Norman Thomas at the Townsend Convention of 1936," **Speech Monographs,** XXIV (November 1957), 234–236. Reprinted with permission.

[3] Most classical rhetoricians, including Aristotle, claimed there were three types of speeches: (1) deliberative; (2) forensic; and (3) epideictic. However, almost all rhetoricians of the period agreed that the general end of speech-making was persuasion.

purpose. He then analyzes the purpose, asking how the speaker adapted his material to the aims suitable for a speech in that category. If the situation called for a speech to convince, it is assumed that the speaker's purpose could be analyzed by asking what belief it was the speaker tried to establish, because all speeches of conviction require the speaker to establish belief.

In many modern speech texts, these categories are referred to as the "general ends" of speech. It is assumed that each general end calls for a certain purpose, e.g., to inform, to entertain, to convince, to stimulate, to actuate. For the critic, this has meant he must determine which category or general end a speech belongs to and then examine the speaker's purpose and means to see if they were adequate to produce the concomitant audience response. In practice, it has been difficult to do this because speeches rarely fit neatly into one of these categories. It is difficult to find a pure informative speech, just as it is difficult to categorize a speech that is designed to move the audience to action as separate and distinct from one intended to stimulate an audience. Sometimes one of these ends will dominate, but more often than not they will overlap.

Two assumptions make this approach to speech purpose difficult to apply: the first, that audience responses are discrete; and the second, that a predetermined set of rhetorical devices can be applied that will produce the desired response. These assumptions appear to be contrary to findings in modern psychology and psycholinguistics, findings that depict human behavior as dynamic and multiplex, with responses resulting from a set or disposition in the individual to react in a certain manner to external stimuli. Thus, what may be informative to one group of people may be convincing to another group. Language, considered neutral in one context, may be inflammatory in a different context.

Such findings tend to discredit any approach that fits speeches into clearly defined and easily separated categories. They suggest that the critic should shift his investigation from examining the speech as a general type to that of examining the speaker's **intent** and the audience's **responses** in light of what **was said** in the speech. Using all three of these factors, the critic would determine the speaker's purpose, both explicit and implicit.

Purpose is more a matter of what the speaker perceives to be his own intent and the demands of the speaking situation than of his selection of a general category of speech to which he then fits his intent and methods. Berlo considers it "more useful to define purpose as the goal of a creator or receiver of a message, rather than as the property of the message itself."[4]

It is better if the critic assumes that the end of every speech is persuasion and that the speaker's purpose will indicate the response he wishes to elicit from his audience. The critic should assume that statements in the speech will reflect the speaker's attempt to **influence** his listeners in a predetermined direction. Even when the ostensible purpose of the speech is solely to inform or produce understanding, the critic should view it as an attempt to influence or persuade the audience to accept the speaker's statements as accurate descriptions of things as they really are. Richard Weaver believes that it is more realistic to consider all speaking as persuasive because: "We see that in all cases the listener is being asked not simply to follow a valid reasoning form but to respond to some presentation of reality. He is being asked to agree with the speaker's interpretation of the world that is."[5] Kenneth Burke puts it another way: "All speech uses Language as a symbolic means of inducing cooperation in beings that by nature respond to symbols. . . . Wherever there is 'meaning' there is 'persuasion.' "[6]

There may be disagreement about the ends and types of speeches men give. But this in no way lessens the demand on the critic to determine the speaker's purpose in every case and to do so in such a way that he understands it in relationship to the audience and the setting. In some speeches, the speaker states his purpose forthrightly for all to hear. In others, the stated purpose is not the speaker's real purpose, and in still others, the speaker does not state purpose or intent in so many words. No matter what overt statements of purpose appear, the critic must ascertain the speaker's actual intent. To do this, he will have to examine the speech itself; and he will have to understand the speaker, the audience, and the occasion to make sure that he has found the basic purpose.

The critic must make a careful investigation of the speech pur-

---

[4] David K. Berlo, **The Process of Communication** (New York: Holt, 1960), p. 10.
[5] Richard M. Weaver, "Language is Sermonic," in **Dimensions of Rhetorical Scholarship,** ed. Roger E. Nebergall (Norman: University of Oklahoma Press, 1963) p. 54.
[6] Kenneth Burke, **A Rhetoric of Motives** (Englewood Cliffs: Prentice-Hall, 1950) p. 172.

pose because at the foundation of rhetoric is the assumption that a significant relationship exists between a communicator's intent and the means by which he communicates. To know the purpose of a communication is to understand the function of the rhetorical devices employed.

The lines of argument

Every speech is an attempt on the part of a speaker to express pertinent ideas so that they will be meaningful, acceptable, and impelling to his hearers. The ideas the speaker chooses to develop will depend largely on his purpose as it relates to his audience and the occasion. If his communication is to be effective in gaining a particular response, the speaker will have to choose his main ideas carefully, put them together so as to provide a unified theme, and develop them in a manner that will permit audience perception. In so doing, the speaker will assert propositions, advance reasons, and offer evidence, all designed to lead to some central idea or conclusion, which, if accepted by the audience, will produce the desired response.

This process comes under the rhetorical canon of **invention.** Invention in rhetoric refers to a method of finding arguments that are appropriate to the subject and audience. It refers to the search for **negotiable** ideas and materials that will enable listeners to see things as the speaker does and value them as he would. To be successful, the speaker must locate arguments that inhere either in the subject or the circumstances surrounding it and present the relevant arguments—those relevant to the subject, the audience, and the speaker's purpose. Arguments are the processes of reasoning wherein the speaker puts together a series of statements and/or evidence in support of a conclusion. If the speaker's process of reasoning is sound and his statements or premises are valid, his argument is usually accepted as proof of the truth of his proposition. When the speaker uses the methods of logic to establish his propositions, it is called logical proof (**logos**); when he uses psychological appeals, emotional proof (**pathos**); and when he uses personal appeals, ethical proof (**ethos**).

The critic must recognize the main propositions in the speech and be able to discern the various proofs used. These two items are basic in every communication. Behind the words the speaker delivers are the propositions the speaker wants to establish and the means by which he hopes to accomplish it. If a speaker wants his audience to believe that the selective service system should be abolished, he will have to locate and develop a series of arguments that will lead the audience from where it is to this new proposition. The speaker will ordinarily need to argue that the present military draft plan is not adequate to meet the needs of modern warfare, that it is unfair in its selection methods, that it creates unnecessary problems and hardships, and that there are already available more effective ways of meeting military-manpower needs. He may press all these arguments or just one or two depending on the existing beliefs and attitudes of the audience, the amount of time he has, and the current status of the controversy. The critic would analyze this speech by investigating the main propositions that form the speaker's case and by understanding the arguments presented in support of these propositions.

Wayne C. Eubank's criticism of Benjamin Morgan Palmer's anti-state-lottery speech, given in Louisiana in 1891, shows the critic at work describing and analyzing the speaker's lines of arguments:

> . . . Near the end of his introduction, Palmer presented the central idea of his speech, "I lay the indictment against the Louisiana Lottery Company that its continued existence is incompatible, not only with the safety, but with the being of the state." Continuing, Palmer declared that he was not "simply uttering the language of denunciation" but that he had framed the indictment and he intended to support each contention with adequate proof.
>
> Palmer opened the main body of the speech by declaring the lottery's legal right to exist comparable to the right of existence of a syndicate to propagate leprosy, a syndicate to extend the advantages of lying, a syndicate to promote murder. . . .
>
> Proceeding to the first main argument upon which he spent about one-half of his time, Palmer denounced the lottery declaring that its existence was contrary to the "first physical matter which forms a basis upon which human society rests . . . the law of labor." Paraphrasing the Biblical phrase "In the sweat of thy brow thou shalt earn thy bread," Palmer maintained that since the creation it had been a fundamental and universal law that each unit of society lived by his individual and personal labor. To illustrate this point, Palmer employed two examples, the farmer and the manufacturer. After extol-

ling the creative virtues of the farmer and the manufacturer, Palmer asked, "what values does the gambler ever create? What new value does he ever stamp upon the value which existed antecedently?" . . .

Continuing the argument Palmer contended that one of the plainest principles of ethics stated that what a man has no right to do, he has no right to bargain to do.

"The man who stakes his property has no right to stake that property on a chance, and the man who won the property upon that stake had no original right to take it. It was neither a gift nor a purchase and consequently the agreement between the parties, to stand simply by the chance, was an immoral agreement and no legislature can possibly make it legitimate."

Proceeding to the second main point in the development of the speech, Palmer denounced the lottery for promoting the principle that some should live upon the losses of those who were unlucky—that the few were enriched through the poverty of the many. He expressed the belief that if the lottery existed for another quarter of a century, much of the wealth of the state would be transferred into the hands of a few. Pronouncing that the people of Louisiana would not tolerate such a condition, Palmer issued the battle cry declaring, "If this lottery cannot be destroyed by forms of law, it must unquestionably be destroyed by actual revolution."

Closing his argument Palmer accused the lottery of becoming the apostle of gambling, a school for instruction in gambling.

"It [the lottery] becomes a propagandist of gambling. It goes forth under the charter of the state to persuade man, woman, child where ever they meet to gamble. It carries the solicitation into our very homes. It meets our cooks when they are going with a basket to get the master's breakfast and induces them to gamble. . . . What I charge, therefore, upon the lottery is not simply that it is a gambling concern but that it is an university for the instruction in gambling."

In advance of his peroration, Palmer pronounced that before half of the twenty-five years had elapsed, if the charter of the lottery were renewed, every citizen able to leave the state would depart. Referring to the bribery tactics of the lottery, Palmer predicted that within ten years after its re-chartering the lottery would carry every governor of the state in its pocket, "remove every honest judge from the bench, and put their men in the places to do their bidding. . . ."[7]

The critic should in every case find the speaker's main arguments, even when they are not clearly identified or fully developed,

[7] Wayne C. Eubank, "Benjamin Morgan Palmer's Lottery Speech, New Orleans, 1891," **The Southern Speech Journal**, XXIV (Fall 1958), 4–6. Reprinted with permission.

Analyzing the speech

because they form the basis of the speech. Arguments and the propositions they support indicate the path by which the speaker intends to lead the audience to his central idea. That these paths or arguments may turn into blind alleys, go in circles, or become obliterated should not deter the critic in his attempt to locate them. Before a speaker can present statistics or analogies or develop emotional appeals, he must have worked out some notion of the proposition he wants established through these means. By describing and analyzing the propositions and arguments as they appear in the speech, the critic will be able to gain insight not only into the basis of the speech itself, but also into the speaker's perception of his communication task.

The modes of proof

Traditionally, rhetoric has concerned itself with the three modes of proof—**logos, pathos, ethos**—recognized as the means by which persuasion is affected. Aristotle defined these proofs as follows:

> . . . The first kind resides in the character of the speaker [**ethos**]; the second consists in producing a certain attitude in the hearer [**pathos**]; the third appertains to the argument proper [**logos**], in so far as it actually or seemingly demonstrates. . . .
>
> The character of the speaker is a cause of persuasion when the speech is so uttered as to make him worthy of belief; . . .
>
> Secondly, persuasion is effected through the audience, when they are brought by the speech into a state of emotion; . . . .
>
> Thirdly, persuasion is effected by arguments, when we demonstrate the truth, real or apparent, by such means as inhere in particular cases.[8]

According to Aristotelian theory, these are the speaker's only means of persuading. If the speaker has ideas, opinions, or premises that he wishes to establish, he must use these modes of proof to make them acceptable to the audience.

Depending on the purpose of the speaker, the type of subject, and the nature of the audience, one of these modes of proof may dominate, but invariably all three will be at work simultaneously throughout the speech. All speakers have to demonstrate the truth of their arguments by logical reasoning (**logos**); they must establish

---

[8] Aristotle, **The Rhetoric,** trans. Lane Cooper (New York: Appleton, 1932), 1356a, 1.2.

that they are worthy of belief because of their character, or competence, or both (**ethos**); and they must arouse listeners to an emotional state in which they will be concerned enough to want to follow the speaker's arguments (**pathos**).

> ... For the most obvious truth about rhetoric is that its object is the whole man. It presents its arguments first to the rational part of the man, because rhetorical discourses, if they are honestly conceived, always have a basis in reasoning. Logical argument is the plot, as it were, of any speech or composition that is designed to persuade. Yet it is the very characterizing feature of rhetoric that it goes beyond this and appeals to other parts of man's constitution, especially to his nature as a pathetic being, that is, a being feeling and suffering. A speech intended to persuade achieves little unless it takes into account how men are reacting subjectively to their special circumstances.[9]

This quotation from Richard Weaver points to the fact that all these modes of proof operate simultaneously. Man is both a rational and an emotional being. In this uncertain world, he must be able to depend upon those who would advise him; and he must have his psychological needs met as well as be convinced through logical demonstration. The speaker who can skillfully bring to bear all three modes of proof in support of a proposition will assuredly be more persuasive. For the critic, this implies that he be able to untangle these webs of proof if he hopes to analyze a speech and account for its effectiveness.

Logical argument. In analyzing a speech, the critic will want to know the logical reasoning used by the speaker. He will want to examine the validity of the reasons and the accuracy of the evidence. The critic will be concerned with the forms of reasoning used by the speaker. He will note fallacies and other inconsistencies in the speaker's argument. The critic will consider also the assumptions on which the logical proof of a speech is based, that is, he will determine the premises granted or assumed in order to check the validity of those propositions presented in the speech. All speeches proceed enthymematically, i.e., the speaker presents a conclusion and one supporting premise, assuming that the audience will supply the other necessary premises. For an enthymeme to be effective, the speaker and audience must be in tacit agreement about the truth of the unstated premises.

[9]Weaver, p. 51.

To illustrate how the critic analyzes logical argument, there follow several excerpts from Donald Streeter's criticism of the speeches of Lucius Q. C. Lamar, a Southern spokesman in the period immediately after the Civil War. Streeter carefully picks out the forms of reasoning used by the speaker, and he assesses the evidence that accompanied this reasoning.

> One of the earliest arguments which Lamar advanced, and to which he returned again and again, was that the South was being misruled. He argued mainly from effect to cause, and brought abundant evidence to support his case. He was particularly apt in the use of quotation from the opposition and from unbiased observers. Having established his case, he suggested his solution: local autonomy in the South. Here he argued from cause to effect, but not as adequately as before, since he based his opinions on what he believed the South would do if given control of its own affairs. What he would have done, and what the South sometimes suggested it might do, in handling the problem of voting privileges, were two different things.
>
> In rising to discuss the report of an investigating committee regarding the alleged causes for the "exodus" of the Negroes from the Southern states, Lamar presented two arguments: That the condition of the Negro in the South was not deplorable, and that if the Negro wanted to migrate to the North, he might profit by the move. The two arguments seem somewhat contradictory. Lamar's proof was adequate in both aspects of his case, however. He quoted voluminous amounts of authority from antislavery sources to show that the condition of the Negro in the South was basically satisfactory, and that great improvement was being made. And he reasoned from cause to effect, based on the Negro's traditional position of subservience in the warm climate of the South, to show that educationally and economically the Negro might improve his lot if he migrated to the North to fill the demand for labor in industry. In other words, he seemed to say that the Negro was doing as well as conditions permitted in the South—that this was better than most people believed—but that in the North, under different conditions, he might do still better.
>
> Lamar's exposure of Republican maladministration in the South was well supported by specific instances, authority, and effect to cause reasoning. However, when he defended what had come to be called the "solid South," he presented rather weak arguments. Rather than show that the solid South had been a benefit to the nation, he attempted to establish that the solidification of Southern political activity had done no harm. He went on to avoid the issue by calling attention to the laws of the State of Minnesota as they might be in-

terpreted to apply to Negroes. Such analogical reasoning was faulty, since neither climate, population, nor the purpose for which the laws were passed made comparison valid.[10]

Ethical proof. Admittedly, the establishment of truth through logical argument is the main function of all communication. Yet the very situations that produce speech-making—doubt, controversy, alternatives, contingencies—frequently make it impossible to produce agreement on truth by reasoning and evidence alone. Knowing this and recognizing that they cannot check all the facts, listeners depend in part on the trustworthiness of the speaker. What the speaker does to produce the feeling that he is knowledgable, of worthy character, and a man of good will is known as **ethical proof.**

In analyzing ethical proofs, the critic considers what the audience knows of the speaker prior to the speech, how the speaker appeared and conducted himself during the speech, what his choice of language reflected about his good taste and his common sense, and in what ways he communicated a sense of sincerity to his hearers. These, and many other factors—such as the use of personal pronouns, references to personal experience, identification with persons of high standing—contribute to the **ethos** of the speaker. The critic must look for the many ways in which a speaker's **ethos** is either increased or lessened in a speech.

Often, a speaker finds himself facing a hostile audience, as in the case of Norman Thomas at the Townsend Convention (discussed earlier in this chapter). In such a case, ethical proof can be of equal importance with logical proof in winning a favorable response from the audience, and the critic must be able to analyze the proofs used by the speaker in adjusting the audience to himself and his ideas. Merwyn Hayes makes this kind of a critical analysis of the speeches of William L. Yancey, a Southerner, who in the Presidential campaign of 1860 made a swing through the Northern states espousing the cause of the South and electioneering for the Southern candidate.

> Keeping in mind Yancey's purpose to prove that he was not a disunionist and to demonstrate that the southern cause was constitution-

[10]Donald C. Streeter, "The Major Public Addresses of Lucius Q. C. Lamar During the Period 1874 to 1890," **Speech Monographs,** XVI (August 1949), 119–121. Reprinted with permission.

ally founded, let us examine exactly what he said. In his introductory remarks Yancey attempted: (a) to establish common ground with his audience, (b) to establish himself as a man of good will, and (c) to signal his audience that the Constitution and the present state of affairs were chiefly what he would be concerned with in his address.

Yancey attempted to establish common ground with his listeners by contending that they were all brothers, for they were all citizens of the same country. At Cooper Institute he said:

"I trust the hour is not yet arrived in which, when an Alabamian speaks to his brothers of the city and State of New York as brothers it will be a subject of jeering and hissing. We ought to be brothers, if we are not. There ought to be a brotherhood of citizenship throughout this vast country which would knit together the social and business relations in bonds so strong that the fanatics of the whole world could not burst them."

In Boston Yancey referred to his boyhood days in New England and the astute training he had received from New England teachers in the Massachusetts schools. Thus a common background served as a device for breaking the ice and establishing common ground upon which both the speaker and the audience stood.

In each of the speeches under consideration, Yancey portrayed himself as a man of high ethical character. Especially true in the introductory remarks, this can also be found throughout the addresses. In Cincinnati he said, "I do not propose to employ the arts of the rhetorician or declaimer, but to reason soberly and truly." In New York he immediately impressed the audience as being straightforward and honest by saying:

". . . I believe, my countrymen, that truth and frankness will win their way at all times to hearts that are swayed by truth, by generosity and by justice. I do not disguise from you—I would not have it otherwise—as a Southern man."

In his introductory remarks Yancey also made it clear that he would defend slavery as a constitutional right. In each of his Northern addresses, he incorporated a statement or two explaining that in order for the Union to be preserved, both the North and the South must rest their faith in the Constitution, a Constitution which insured the right of slavery.[11]

In addition to those elements within the speech that are planned by the speaker to produce ethical proof, there are factors outside

[11]Merwyn A. Hayes, "William L. Yancey Presents the Southern Case to the North, 1860," **The Southern Speech Journal**, XXIX (Spring 1964), 202–204. Reprinted with permission.

the speech itself that affect the speaker's **ethos.** Some of these things the speaker has control over, others he does not. Yet they all add to the composite that creates the image of the speaker for the audience. Herold Truslow Ross analyzes some of these "outside" ethical factors in his evaluation of a speech by Senator Albert J. Beveridge on the disposition of the Philippine Islands after the Spanish-American War.

> As the noon hour approached on Tuesday, January 10, and the morning business was drawing to a close, the galleries of the Senate chamber began to fill rapidly. Beveridge's announcement that he would speak at this time had been given wide publicity and had occasioned much comment, especially in Washington. The undoubted understanding known to exist between the Senator and President McKinley in the White House gave the proposed utterance the status of an administration pronouncement. The public was also curious as to the information that Beveridge had collected on his visit to the islands and withheld so long. Many also wished to hear his maiden speech in the Senate. His wide reputation as a speaker had grown upon the consistency of his eloquence. In Congressional circles there was not only interest but amazement that a new member of the Senate should break the tradition of the conscript fathers and make an important speech before he had passed through a year of silence. The very audacity of the act, however, drew them to the chamber for the enactment of the scene. . . . Senator Beveridge arose and asked for the reading of his resolution. Instantly the animated undertone of conversation quieted. With a slow, sweeping glance about him at his audience, he began:
>
> "Mr. President: I address the Senate at this time because Senators and Members of the House on both sides have asked that I give to Congress and the country my observations in the Philippines and the Far East, and the conclusions which these observations compel; and because of hurtful resolutions introduced and utterances made in the Senate, every word of which will cost and is costing the lives of American soldiers." . . .
>
> Slight of form, short of stature, smooth of face, looking ten years younger than his age . . . speaking rapidly in a voice clear and musical as a silver bell, with an enunciation perfectly distinct, and in tones modulated to suit each particular phase of his remarks, the new Senator from Indiana won such a triumph as seldom comes to any public man. His manner was earnest, his delivery graceful, his few gestures, timely and effective. At intervals he drove home telling

points with passionate fervor and dramatic force, but for the most part he employed the conversational mode. . . .[12]

Emotional proof. Just as the speaker's manner, appearance, tone of voice, sincerity, good judgment, and character move the audience to accept his message, so do the means by which the speaker involves the audience's emotions impell them to react in the desired direction. The means the speaker employs to make his auditors favorably disposed psychologically toward his ideas are called **emotional proof.** These are sometimes designated the psychological proofs, as contrasted with the logical proofs. They are the appeals to human desires and needs that fire the imagination and arouse the will.

The critic in analyzing speeches for emotional proof gives careful consideration to the audience, for it is the **adaptation** of the speaker's materials to his particular audience that produces the favorable emotional disposition. The critic is concerned with **how** the speaker makes the necessary adjustments in argument, example, and language to his hearers that will favorably dispose them toward his purpose. Whether the speaker has created emotional proof purposely or not, the critic knows that the reaction to a speech is the reaction of the whole man—not just a man's logical but also his psychological responses. Consequently, the critic examines the speaker's choices of materials for the kinds of emotional responses they are likely to produce in the audience, whether the speaker planned for them or not. The point here is that all of us respond emotionally to language, and these responses when controlled by the speaker can greatly aid his communication, and when left to chance can greatly hamper his efforts.

Turning once again to Vasilew's criticism of the Thomas speech at the Townsend Convention, one can see how he analyzes the psychological proofs in that speech:

> Appeals to democracy and fair play were among the most effective pathetic devices Thomas employed in this speech. He began with them in his introduction, and carried them into his first digression. ". . . isn't it fair in America that minority parties should be on the ballot without such difficulties as to make it impossible?" he asked.

---

[12]Herold Truslow Ross, "Albert J. Beveridge," **A History and Criticism of American Public Address,** Vol. II, ed. W. N. Brigance (New York: McGraw-Hill, 1943), p. 931. Used with permission of McGraw-Hill Book Co.

His second digression was also concerned with democracy in so far as he argued against the right of the Supreme Court to negate Congress' legislative powers. He declared, "There is no defense of a democracy which leaves the final decisions in matters of this sort [social legislation] to a court, to a majority of nine men who sit on the Supreme Court."

Much later in the speech he returned to these appeals when he digressed again to speak of Father Coughlin's attack on Roosevelt. ". . . I do not think America is going to be helped by a campaign of personal hate and bitterness," he said, and the audience cheered him.

The remainder of Thomas' pathetic appeals were directed mainly to the special interests of the hearers. Urging them to support a constitutional amendment which would allow Congress to pass economic and social legislation not subject to court review, he warned that the Townsend Plan itself would never be enacted unless the power of the Supreme Court was thus abrogated. When he asked his hearers to support socialism, he reminded them that Socialists have always favored bigger old age pensions.

He used emotional proof skillfully in a figurative analogy which argued against the Townsend Plan as a cure-all for America's economic ills. He said: "My friends—Dr. Townsend is a physician. There must have been many times when a man came to him with tuberculosis and wouldn't admit it, and some friend said, 'Just try this cough drop and you will be all right,' and Dr. Townsend I suspect said, 'My friend, I am sorry for you, you can get well, but you cannot do it by this cough drop' . . . I tell you that you can get well, but you cannot get well under the capitalist system by this particular method."[13]

Organization

Closely allied to the inventional aspects of a speech are the organizational ones that produce the order and form of the speech. In oral discourse, organization plays an extremely important part. It is usual for the speaker to lead the audience from some already established point to a new or different conclusion by a series of steps or arguments that lead obviously to the desired conclusion. This order of ideas and materials plays a significant role in the achievement of the speaker's goals. Should his listeners become confused or misled because of poor organization, the speaker's central point could become lost, no matter how well-developed his arguments and proofs.

[13]Vasilew, p. 238. Reprinted with permission.

Analyzing the speech

A critical analysis of the arrangement of a speech is important to the critic because it is one of the best methods for discovering the strategies employed by the speaker. Not only will the critic want to examine the basic plan of the speech to find the steps leading to the conclusion, but he will want also to analyze the arrangement to see how ideas are made important by where they are placed in the speech. And, as with arguments and proofs, the analysis of the order of the speech will reveal how the speaker adapted to the audience's knowledge and attitudes.

For an example of a speaker's use of arrangement to adapt his materials to his purpose, examine the analysis of Daniel Webster's "Adams and Jefferson" address in Faneuil Hall, August 2, 1826. Wilbur Howell and Hoyt Hudson state that:

> The plan of the speech shows admirable symmetry and proportion. After an extended introduction, which dwells upon the coincidence of their deaths and traces the parallelism of their lives, Webster tells (1) the biography of Adams up to the meeting of the first Continental Congress and then (1') more briefly, the same portion of Jefferson's story. This brings him to the longest single section, (2) an account of the inception, drafting, and voting of the Declaration, with emphasis upon Jefferson's part in the drafting and Adams's part in winning the vote. After a brief digression praising four other signers, (3) the life of Adams after 1776 is recounted summarily, and (3') the same is done for Jefferson. Jefferson's founding of the University of Virginia leads to (4) an estimate of the scholarly and literary attainments of the two men, followed by (5) a judgment upon their administrations as President, with enforcement of the controlling idea, namely, that though opposed in policies and principles, the two were at one in serving their country and maintaining the Constitution; and this section is closed by a brief peroration to the eulogy proper. The speech could have ended here, but it would have lacked something of general application. After a short digression in praise of Charles Carroll, the only surviving signer of the Declaration, Webster delivers the peroration of the whole address, urging that Americans may appreciate their heritage and "resolve to maintain and perpetuate it." The speech took little more than two hours in delivery, with section 2, on the Declaration, occupying 45 minutes. The moving exposition of "true eloquence" comes exactly at the middle and is followed by the vivid dramatization of a session of the Continental Congress, with a speech

by an unnamed opponent of independence and Adams's longer reply. Thus was the audience stirred and refreshed, in preparation for nearly fifty minutes of speaking yet to come.[14]

Style

Style, in the classical or Aristotelian tradition, is considered the third cannon of rhetoric. It occupied this position because it was assumed that after the speaker had located his arguments and proofs, and had arranged them in some effective order, he then turned his attention to clothing them in eloquent language. Style was viewed as the process in which the speaker chose his words and composed them so as to give the most effective expression to his thoughts.

If one follows this tradition and attempts to treat style as separate from thought, he will have problems as a critic. For example, it is difficult to conceive of **pathos**—emotional proof—as separate from the language that expresses it because, more often than not, it is the language itself that signals the emotional response in the hearer. Or, consider **ethos;** the audience feeling toward the speaker may in large part be determined by the language he uses. It is extremely difficult for the critic in his analysis and evaluation of a speech to treat invention and style as separate and distinct categories. Often it will be impossible to distinguish thought from the language that expresses it, and the critic may be hard pressed to explain which one accounts for the audience response.

Despite the interrelatedness of thought and language, there are qualities of style over which the speaker has control, and the choices he makes in these areas of language definitely affect his speech. These qualities have long been known as **correctness, clearness, appropriateness,** and **ornateness.** Each one refers to a particular aspect of language or composition that governs the choices a person makes in his attempt to produce meaning and impact. The critic can assess these stylistic choices and make some judgment about their effectiveness.

It would be impossible within the confines of this chapter to

[14]Wilbur Samuel Howell and Hoyt Hudson, "Daniel Webster," Vol. I, ed. W. N. Brigance (New York: McGraw-Hill, 1943), pp. 683–684. Used with permission of the publisher.

Analyzing the speech

explore the tremendous number of constituents of style and consider what they mean for the speech critic. No doubt all of them have something to do with the effect a speech produces. There is no escape from the fact that imagery, metaphor, hyperbole, alliteration, rhythm, perspicuity, and taste all play a vital role in communication. Language that is inappropriately ornate can alienate an audience, whereas language carefully suited to the subject and occasion, enriched with figures and a flowing rhythm, can embellish human thought.

Style is the most complex and the most creative constituent of communication, and therefore the most difficult for the critic to analyze. The best the critic can hope for is to locate that aspect of style or those qualities of style that most distinguish the particular speech or speaker under consideration and then assess their value in relating the speaker's thoughts to his hearers.

Below are excerpts from two criticisms; each emphasizes a different aspect of style. In the first, the critic is concerned with the speaker's word choice and composition. In the second, the critic examines style as it is related to the speaker's delivery.

Herman Stelzner, in analyzing those attributes of style that account for John Morley's success as a British Parliamentary speaker, states:

> One quality of style which contributed to his success was his choice and use of language. Churchill comments that the "pageantry as well as the distinction of words" arrested attention, and Murray notes his "exact and completely unaffected" style. When Morley used abstract terminology it was usually followed by a series of explanatory phrases, which left little doubt of his meaning and the extent to which he committed himself. Because he disliked "using violent and strong language" he tempered critical remarks. He preferred the phrase "greatly mistaken" to "absolutely false" when addressing himself to colleagues' proposals. . . . Morley insisted on precision in language usage because the "qualifications are consistently the most significant parts of speeches."

Morley ordered his words as carefully as he chose them. By introducing a word or a phrase with a qualifying statement he directed the listeners' attention to the idea he wanted to emphasize. Two passages, selected arbitrarily, illustrate the effectiveness of his sentence construction:

> "It is lamentable . . . to think how the one great single industry (agriculture) of Ireland has been, if I may be pardoned for using the term, bedevilled, by the levity and shortsightedness of Parliament after Parliament."
>
> "These pledges (made by Conservatives)—and I am not using language which I am not prepared to stand by—these pledges have been betrayed."
>
> In these two quotations the key words are "bedeviled" and "betrayed." The importance of the word order to Morley's purpose can be illustrated by re-arranging the components of the second statement to make it read: "These pledges have been betrayed, and I am not using language which I am not prepared to stand by." In this compound sentence the emphasis is dissipated by the conjunction, "and"; thus it lacks the directive influence and force of Morley's statement.
>
> Morley's speeches are also marked by vigorous and apt descriptions; his aphorisms and epigrams quickly earned him a "reputation for happy phrases." After the Lords rejected Gladstone's Reform Bill in 1884, Morley commented that the only solution was "to mend them, or end them," a phrase which became a rallying cry for those who endorsed reform. Exclamatory statements abound in his addresses. They not only supplied additional force and energy, but they indicated his strong feelings about policies and actions. . . .
>
> The importance of diction and sentence structure to Morley's purpose is demonstrated again in this passage. "Sealed the book of knowledge," "strip them of the fruits of their toil," "Friend and comforter in the dark hour," elevate his thought. Morley might have written the passage with two assertions, omitting the conditional clauses: they were often ignorant; it was your laws. . . . They were poor; it was your laws. . . . But this construction is harsher, sharper, and blunter than Morley's. It has a tone of a charge rather than a plea; and the tone is not compatible with that of the ethical commonplace, "Do the Irish as you would be done by."[15]

This final example of analysis of style is also an analysis of the speaker's delivery—another canon of rhetoric—again demonstrating the interrelatedness of all rhetorical constituents. J. Jeffery Auer analyzes the speaking of Tom Corwin, the Ohio Congressman, who earned the epithet "King of the Stump" because of his frontier manner of speaking.

> In manner of delivery, first of all, the stump speaker tended to an

[15]Herman Stelzner, "The British Orators, VII; John Morley's Speechmaking," **The Quarterly Journal of Speech,** XLV (April 1959), 179–181. Reprinted with permission.

exaggerated and declamatory style. Though Corwin apparently relied less than some of his fellows upon vocal noise and vehemence it was said of him that "never had a speaker more complete control over his voice, or voice more power over an audience." Within a few sentences "it would often expand from the lowest conversational tone, audible only in the speaker's immediate vicinity, to a climax which would startle his thousands of hearers in the remotest galleries." Even Rufus Choate confessed that Corwin "would fill the cup of your eyes with tears in a single sentence." More than upon his voice, however, Corwin relied upon gestures and facial expression to entertain and persuade his hearers. . . .

In his general style of speaking Corwin, like most stump orators of the period, was more conversational htan didactic, demonstrative rather than deliberative. Western oratory was admittedly verbose and intumescent and, though Corwin perhaps tried to avoid these extremes by absorbing the moderate tone of the great British orators whose speeches he often read over before an effort of his own, his speaking was usually extempore, and when on the stump he tended to rely more heavily upon a seemingly inexhaustible supply of anecdotes, historical allusions, illustrations, and droll stories than upon closely-knit argument. . . .

From his arsenal of oratorical weapons Tom Corwin, like most stump speakers of his day, most often drew the broad-sword of humor, the rapier of imagery, and the dagger of invective. In the use of each he was unexcelled, entertaining his audience with witty anecdotes, carrying his argument by rhetorical flights of fancy, and excoriating his opponents with sarcasm and ridicule. Perhaps Corwin's greatest strength on the stump was that he entertained as well as instructed; he "put a principle or a reason in the form of a jest so that it would go farther than even eloquence could carry it with the whimsical Western people." His jests might be at the expense of an opponent in the campaign, simple humorous and relevant stories, or even bits of self-satire. . . .

The florid and fanciful images, spacious, rhythmical and vivid, which marked the language of the Western lawyer before a jury of twelve men were carried over by the stump speaker before a political rally of thousands. Corwin's speeches were filled with such references as he once made to Benjamin Franklin, "the philosopher of America who played with the forked lightning of heaven as a child plays with a tamed snake." In his legislative speaking he drew heavily upon Milton, Byron, Dryden, Gibbon, and other classicists for allusions and illustrations, but when he spoke from the stump Corwin turned more often to the Bible for his imagery, employing the language of the prophets of old with a fervor of his own. When an illustration proved itself effective he used it time and again in his speaking, even many years later; he was continually polishing and adding to his stock of favorite images, illustrations, and historical anecdotes, so that he might blend humor and pathos into his "rare dramatic faculty" so much admired by Charles Sumner.[16]

Delivery

Auer's critical analysis of Tom Corwin's speaking reveals the part that delivery plays in speech. He comments on the facial expressions, gesture, appearance, tone of voice, and manner of presentation, and he assumes that all played a part as instruments of persuasion in Corwin's speech-making.

Delivery, like style, is difficult to treat separately from the other constituents of speech. Auer's criticism reveals how closely related it is to style. It can easily be recognized that factors such as physical appearance and fluency play an important role in ethical proof, whereas tone of voice and inflections are extremely important to the creation of emotional response. The speaker's dress, bodily action, and use of the voice are all part of the speech, yet these alone seldom produce persuasion. All are important, but only as each aids the speaker in imparting his message to his hearers.

Further complicating analysis of delivery is the fact that this is the only constituent of a speech that cannot be found in the speech manuscript. The critic must either see the speech delivered or rely upon accounts produced by others. If he was not present, the critic must delve into newspaper accounts and memoirs, as Auer did, in order to make an analysis. This may mean that older speeches and those delivered to small audiences will be only incompletely analyzed and evaluated because of a lack of information. In any case, the critic must do what he can to assess the delivery of a speech accurately so that he may better understand why the audience responded as it did. He must determine its suitability to the material presented and the needs of the occasion; its intelligibility; its agreeableness to the eye and the ear; its impact on the audience.

The critical analysis of a speech is an exacting task. It requires

[16] J. Jeffery Auer, "Tom Corwin: 'King of the Stump,'" **The Quarterly Journal of Speech,** XXX (February 1944), 52–54. Reprinted with permission.

use of all the usual research tools of the scholar, as well as his patience in ferreting out detail, open-mindedness in seeing things as they really are, and discipline in carrying the task to completion in an orderly fashion. It requires, also, a knowledge of the rhetorical canons of invention, arrangement, style, and delivery, so that none of the facets of a speech will escape the critic's scrutiny. Only after he has made a careful and complete analysis of a speech is he in a position to make judgments that bear the stamp of authority.

FOUR

Interpreting the speech

A careful analysis of a speech provides the critic with a firm grasp of what has been said, to whom, under what circumstances, and why. After the critic has revealed the speech in this way, he is ready to move into the area of critical judgment. He is ready to begin his **appraisal** of the speech as a worthy artistic effort. This requires that he form opinions and make judgments. He must make inferences about the meaning and the effects of the various rhetorical constituents employed. In other words, the critic has to **interpret** what took place, and in so doing he makes subjective assessments of what he has analyzed.

To the question, "What is interpretation?" I. A. Richards responded, "Inference and guess work! What else is interpretation? How, apart from inference and skilled guess work, can we be supposed ever to understand a writer or speaker's thought?"[1] By inference and skilled guess work, the critic interprets the speech and establishes the basis for his value judgments of the speech. To accomplish this, the critic must know not only rhetorical forms and techniques, but also audiences and the historical settings that bring the speaker and audience together. It is not enough that the critic locate and label rhetorical devices, such as argument, emotional appeal, imagery, and so forth. He must see these as interactions among the speaker, audience, and occasion, and he must assess their **meaning** in that dynamic situation.

[1] I. A. Richards, **The Philosophy of Rhetoric** (New York: Oxford University Press, 1936), p. 53.

The forms or techniques of rhetoric have no values in themselves. They are useful to the critic only as tools for analyzing the speech and understanding the possible meanings of the form-content units of the speech. Finding examples of standard rhetorical devices is of no help unless the critic can discover and interpret their uniqueness in a particular communicative situation.

The critic is concerned, in the interpretive phase of criticism, with **function** and **meaning**. He wants to understand how the speaker's ideas were translated into form and technique and what meaning these things have for the situation in which they are applied. He looks for **adaptability** and **suitability** of forms. He wants to know how the speaker adapted to the rhetorical problem and how suitable his methods were to his subject, audience, and occasion. To arrive at these interpretations, the critic must draw inferences about the meaning and effect of what took place.

The speaker

Important to any criticism is an understanding of the artist or, in this situation, the speaker. Because speech is an attempt by the speaker to bring about definite responses to some specific concept of his, it is important to know about his process of thought and value systems. A speaker is confronted with a specific urgency; and what he chooses to do about it, or how he chooses to make his desired order come true, is determined by his training and experience, his perception of the world and those who inhabit it, his habits of thought, and his language patterns.

A knowledge of psychology and the findings of experimental psychologists will prove most helpful to the critic in analyzing the speaker and interpreting his statements. Since the time of Freud, psychologists have been providing an ever-increasing knowledge of human behavior that is useful to the critic in his analysis of a speaker's motives and his environmental conditioning. What a man says is most assuredly determined by what he is psychologically, and the meaning of his utterances can be best understood if the critic uses techniques similar to those of the psychologist.[2]

---

[2] Two examples of works devoted to psychological approaches to communication are Carl I. Hovland, Irving L. Janis, and Harold H. Kelley, **Communication and Persuasion: Psychological Studies of Opinion Change** (New Haven: Yale University Press, 1953) and J. A. C. Brown **Techniques of Persuasion** (Baltimore: Penguin Books, 1963).

The critic attains information on the speaker's background, his training, his vocation, his beliefs, and his philosophy. Using his psychological understanding, the critic makes interpretations of the speaker's choice of topic, selection of purpose, form of argument, modes of proof, use of language, and manner of delivery. The sum of a man's psychological experiences determines the way he perceives the world, and this perception influences the choices he makes as he tries to induce others to see the world as he does. The critic must know the speaker as a person and be able to interpret or give meaning to the speaker's rhetorical choices as the speaker conceived of them. In this way, the critic makes skilled inferences about the speaker's intent.

Thus, Charles F. Hunter explains the meaning of some of Thomas Hart Benton's speech methods through interpretation of his philosophical beliefs:

> In determining the precepts upon which Benton based his thinking, we are at once impressed with several practices of the man. First, and foremost, one cannot help being struck by the amount of information which he presented, information which, from all evidences, he had completely mastered. The amount was so great and the practice so widespread that one immediately questions why a speaker, over a long period of years, would persist in the delivery of such minute and carefully selected factual material. . . .
>
> The answer to our query lies in the fundamental philosophy of Benton. He imputed worthy motives to people—he could hardly have done less since his own were irreproachable—but he was then under the necessity of accounting for the opposition to his own ideas and action. If he were right, how could intelligent, high-minded people disagree? The answer is obvious: Their information was shallow or incorrect; they had formed their opinions on too few basic facts; their generalizations were hasty, and as a result their reasoning could not be valid. How then change their minds and mold their opinions to conform with his own? By presenting almost every iota of information that bore upon the particular subject. Then, it followed, a high-minded, righteous-thinking audience would accept his position and adopt his proposal. Naturally, this concept would not apply to every issue, and he was aware of it; opinion, for instance, was molded by many things other than facts or figures. But his speeches on the public lands, on the national bank, on the money question, on Texas, on Oregon, and on the railroads clearly illustrate the principle. The more

learning and knowledge that one possessed on a subject, then the more capable was he of forming an opinion and adopting a line of action. The speaker's task, after he had once convinced himself by prodigious labor that a view was right, was to present the fruits of his study and research. . . .

There is evident in Benton, also, a certain lawyer-like attitude toward the solution of problems. He was by no means interested in abstract thought or in any great visionary themes of reform. In fact, one questions whether he was able to follow long trains of abstract thought; he intensely disliked Calhoun's architectural skill in this branch. But there is almost no department of knowledge touching the practical life of his fellow men that he did not seek to master. All through his active congressional life, his cry was, "Give us the facts. What are the facts?" And it was only after he knew and had mastered them that he proceeded to discuss them. In this approach there is an almost complete disregard for the individual or for the personality. In none of his speeches do we find any emphasis upon the effects or benefits accruing to the individual as a result of his measures. One feels that after the basic premises of good and evil, of justice and injustice had been settled in the speaker's mind, there was nothing left to consider. This outlook is essentially legal. It is certainly not the viewpoint of the minister, or the doctor, or the psychologist, or the politician; they are concerned primarily with the individual. For Benton, the greatest measure of success of any proposal was the ultimate prestige and prosperity of the nation. The individual as such is almost ignored.[3]

Through Hunter's interpretations, one acquires an understanding of Benton's approach to his speeches, his repetition of certain arguments, and the positions he took on the important issues of his time. Through this understanding of the man and his beliefs, the critic is better able to appraise Benton's speech-making and judge its effect.

The audience

A key word in rhetorical theory is **adaptation.** A speech is a process of adaptation or adjustment, of adjusting ideas to men and men to ideas. In the symbolic processes of speech, there can be no direct transference of thought or perception from the speaker to the

[3]Charles F. Hunter, "Thomas Hart Benton: An Evaluation," **The Quarterly Journal of Speech,** XXX (October 1944), 282–284. Reprinted with permission.

hearer. The speaker must find means by which he can adapt his understanding of the good or the expedient to the understanding of his audience. These means of audience adaptation in discourse can be analyzed and described by the critic in terms of the rhetorical constituents identified in Chapter 3. The effects produced in hearers by these rhetorical means of adaptation can be **interpreted** by the critic if he knows about the audience and the way in which it is likely to respond to the speaker's adaptations.

To know audiences, the critic must know something about our society; its structures; its values; its modes of thought and conduct. Here again, psychological studies and sociological studies, as well, can aid the critic in understanding why audiences respond as they do. The members of the audience have their motives just as the speaker does, and their behavior can also be explained psychologically. Further, the findings of the sociologist regarding why people join the groups they do, how groups condition their thinking and acting, and how and why they respond as they do to authority figures are invaluable to the critic in his interpretations of audience effect in the speaking situation.[4]

In the final analysis, the success of a communication is dependent upon audience response. It is dependent on the author's treatment of his audience rather than on his treatment of his subject. For a speech to be effective, the speaker has to align his arguments, proofs, and language with his hearers' thoughts. To do this, he utilizes the **resources within the audience.** The critic makes his interpretations in this area of interaction between speaker and audience. He must understand audiences and recognize the part they play in shaping the speech and in giving meaning to the speaker's rhetorical choices. Wrage and Baskerville express this point well in their volume on American speeches:

> . . . although a speech is primarily expressive of the mind of the speaker, it also is a gauge to the mind of the audience, both listeners and readers. What speakers choose to talk about and what listeners choose to listen to are matters esteemed by both parties. In still other

[4]As examples of widely differing volumes which have value for the speech critic in understanding audience behavior see Lyman Bryson, ed., **The Communication of Ideas** (New York: Harper, 1948); Carolyn Sherif, Muzafer Sherif, and Roger Nebergall, **Attitude and Attitude Change** (Philadelphia: Saunders, 1965); Bernard M. Bass, **Leadership, Psychology, and Organizational Behavior** (New York: Harper, 1960).

ways a speech bears the impress of an audience, always covertly, often overtly. Through intuition, experience or by precept, effective public speakers discover they must take into account the interests, belief-systems, prejudices, and caprices of their audiences. The adaptations speakers make are implicit in the formulations of their arguments in idiomatic language, in images fashioned from life experiences of the group, and in appeals that go to the heart as well as the head.[5]

Criticism is not simply a matter of pointing out how and why the speaker used such devices as logical proof, emotional proof, and metaphorical language in achieving his purpose. An argument or an appeal could be excellent in its revelation of the subject matter and suitable to the speaker's interests, yet be ineffectual in generating a desirable response. Merely pointing out the use of such an argument or appeal without interpreting its effect on the audience would not reveal all its potential meanings.

To understand how well the speaker utilizes the resources available in the audience is important to the assessment of any speech. Because all speech-making is an **interaction** between the speaker and the hearers, speech-making cannot be appraised without interpretation of the part the audience plays in this interaction. One means of understanding this interaction is to understand the enthymemes used in the speech.

Rhetoricians since Aristotle have recognized that speech is enthymematic in form and function rather than dialetic. The success of a communication depends on the hearer to supply certain **omitted** premises and evidences as the speaker unfolds his argument. If a speaker says, "I want you to drive carefully because we must stop this senseless slaughter on our highways," he is counting on his hearers supplying a whole series of "missing" premises, such as, "everyone who drives wants to avoid accidents," "highway accident deaths can be prevented," "accidents are caused by careless drivers," "careful driving can stop accidents." He expects that listeners will supply these assumed premises and that they will produce evidence from their own experience and knowledge to clarify and validate statements like "this senseless slaughter." To the degree that the speaker's statements call forth the needed premises from within the audience, i.e., to the degree that he uses effectively enthy-

[5]Ernest J. Wrage and Barnet Baskerville, eds., **American Forum: Speeches on Historic Issues, 1788–1900** (New York: Harper, 1960), pp. vii–ix.

memes, his communication will involve his hearers with him in a joint development of thought that results in the acceptance of the conclusion desired by the speaker. If the speaker cannot produce this kind of involvement, his efforts are likely to prove sterile no matter how correct his logic. For the critic, unfolding and interpreting this enthymematic function in a speech is vital to his assessment of the speech.

Understanding the dynamic relationship between speaker and audience is important to the critic in another way. Every speech is a **confrontation,** involving both the speaker's world and the audience's world. This confrontation forces the speaker to adjust his own thoughts and language in order to bring about a reconciliation of differences. The critic must see the audience not simply as a receiver of the speech's form and content, but rather as an agent that affects the speaker's perceptions and choices. Raymond A. Bauer, who has studied this phenomenon, concludes his findings with the statement:

> . . . the audience does not operate independently either of the content of the information in question or of the communicator's values. In some instances the communicator apparently accommodated his image of the audience so as to reduce the perceived incongruence between it and his values and information.[6]

The critic, like the speaker, needs to understand the audience that provides the **raison d'être** for the speech. Whatever meaning a speech has, it has in terms of the audience that responds to it. This is demonstrated in Carroll C. Arnold's study of the speaking career of George William Curtis. Curtis was a literary commentator and lecturer in the last half of the nineteenth century who rose to fame as a speaker on the lyceum circuit. Arnold provides a careful analysis of Curtis' audiences and an assessment of the interaction that existed:

> The lyceum of the fifties and sixties offered Curtis an ideal opportunity to enlighten the unenlightened and to arouse the educated to their social duties. . . .
>
> Of what sort were these thousands who heard Curtis lecture? What expectations and inclinations did they bring to the lecture hall? "You

---

[6]Raymond A. Bauer, "The Communicator and the Audience," in **People, Society, and Mass Communication,** eds. L. A. Dexter and D. M. White (New York: Free Press of Glencoe, 1964), pp. 133–134.

will find," said an anonymous writer who may have been Curtis himself, "that the lecture audience is composed mainly of young people, and largely of women." Later, Curtis recorded his belief that those who gathered in the lecture halls were "all profoundly interested in the moral principles which were involved in the political situation." In both judgments Curtis' views have modern support. The general desire for self-culture, which characterized the age, "was often associated with a somewhat vague feeling that the acquisition of culture was in itself a satisfaction and that it further enhanced the value of living," according to Curtis. And another student of the time has added a qualification which is also reflected in the observations appearing in **Putnam's** and the "Editor's Easy Chair":

"The American's attitude toward culture was at once suspicious and indulgent. Where it interfered with more important activities, he distrusted it; where it was the recreation of his leisure hours or of his womenfolk, he tolerated it. For the most part, he required that culture serve some useful purpose."

The nineteenth-century lecture hall was at once a monument to cultural aspiration and a public forum. Those who purchased tickets for the lecture "courses" did so, at least in part, out of a yearning for significant knowledge. By an act of will they presented themselves before the lecturer. They expected some reward for their efforts. Some sought release from their uncertainties, some desired reinforcement for their predispositions, some desired solace for their feelings of cultural inadequacy; others undoubtedly sought no more than satisfaction for their curiosity or relief from a humdrum existence. Almost none, however, could be satisfied by an offering of either culture for culture's sake or entertainment for entertainment's sake. The lyceum, in its second phase, was what **Putnam's** observer called it: "a weekday church a little humanized." Its members expected enlightenment and inspiration.

George William Curtis met perfectly the expectations of such audiences as these. His own view of what a lecture should be coincided exactly with what lyceum audiences seem to have demanded. Said he:

"An American popular lecture is a brisk sermon upon the times. Whatever its nominal topic may be, the substance of the discourse is always cognate to this people and this age. It may be a critical, a historical, or a moral discourse; but it is relished by the audience just in the degree that it is applied to them. . . .

"The lyceum in this country has been emphatically what it has been so often called—lay preaching. . . ."

In the lyceum and in academic halls Curtis was fortunate in finding audiences generally interested in what he wanted most to give them—genteel sermons on the times. As a political speaker he was not always equally fortunate. . . .

Men sharing less common ground with the speaker must have found it difficult to forget in a few minutes the many ways in which Curtis always showed that he was and wished to be the spokesman for the social and moral views of a class. James Ford Rhodes has probably drawn an accurate description of Curtis' potentialities as a campaign speaker and, by implication, specified his limitations in this form of public address. Says the admiring Rhodes, referring specifically to the Wesleyan University speech cited above:

"To college men, and men who read much, it spoke with mighty accents. The sincere and thoughtful orator had an earnest purpose; he looked upon politics from a lofty plane. . . . The voter who was influenced by that argument must have felt that he had been borne into a political atmosphere which was freed from foul exhalations." In short, if one may judge from his Wesleyan University speech, from his address in behalf of Cleveland's candidacy, and from news reports and other accounts of his campaign speaking, it appears that he consistently addressed himself to the same classes of men who were his admirers in the lecture halls. With that segment of his campaign audience, and probably with that segment only, he was eminently successful.[7]

Carroll Arnold's interpretation of the effectiveness of Curtis' speaking is based upon his appraisal of Curtis' ideas and appeals and their suitability or unsuitability to the various audiences Curtis confronted. A quite different interpretation of a speaker-audience relationship can be found in Ernest G. Bormann's criticism of Huey Long's national radio broadcasts during the Great Depression of the 1930's. Bormann is concerned with the speaker's motives and the means he used to manipulate audience response to his own ends.

> The Kingfish did not begin his radio campaign with overt appeals to increase his own prestige. In this regard he failed to follow the advice of Aristotle, who said, "When a defendant is about to present his case, he must dislodge whatever stands in his way, and so any prejudice against him must be removed at the outset."

[7]Carroll D. Arnold, "George William Curtis," in **A History and Criticism of American Public Address**, Vol. III, ed. Marie Hochmuth (New York: Longmans, 1955), pp. 140–147. © 1965 Russell & Russell Inc. Reprinted by permission.

Long was supposedly defending his "Share Our Wealth" plan, yet he did not try to remove the prejudice against him at outset of his radio broadcasts. Why did he reverse the traditional procedure? The answer can be found in the purpose that motivated him. He was not really interested in implementing the "Share Our Wealth" plan. What he was actually interested in was gaining the personal allegience of his listeners. He needed to overcome the negative aspects of his reputation to do so, and these radio broadcasts were designed to accomplish just that. He was trying to solve not an economic problem but a rhetorical problem with this plan. The speaker, embarked on a campaign for the presidency, was faced with the age-old political task of making himself a popular personage. To make himself popular and politically successful Huey Long decided that he needed a plan which was plausible, simple and powerful in motive appeal. His answer was the "Share Our Wealth" plan. As an economic program for a depression-ridden country the "Share Our Wealth" plan was shot full of holes; as a rhetorical device to make him popular and appeal to the desires of his audience, the plan was a masterpiece as its effectiveness testifies.[8]

The occasion

Closely related to, if not inseparable from, analysis and interpretation of the audience effects is consideration of the **occasion** that gives rise to the speech. It is axiomatic that speech occurs at a specific time and place in history. Further, every speech occurs as a product of the times or cultural milieu that produce the conditions that make the speech necessary. Neither the flaccid appeals of a George Curtis nor the demagogic harangues of a Huey Long can be adequately evaluated apart from the times in which they occur. Lincoln's "with malice toward none, with charity for all," may have a certain timelessness about it, but its rhetorical meaning can be adequately interpreted only in terms of a nation bound in a deadly civil war.

Adequate assessment of the times can be a difficult assignment for the critic, particularly for speeches of the past. The critic is also a product of his time, and it requires a high degree of diligence and objectivity on his part to set aside the prevailing moods of his own

[8] Ernest G. Bormann, "A Rhetorical Analysis of the National Radio Broadcasts of Senator Huey Pierce Long," **Speech Monographs,** XXIV (November 1957), 255–257. Reprinted with permission.

time in order to understand those of another time and place. But this is exactly what the critic must do, if he is to grasp the full meaning of the speech and understand its effects on the audience.

Historical time is reflected both in what the speaker talks about and in his mode of handling his subject. It is also influential on audience response. Many otherwise meritorious speeches have been found wanting because they were either ahead of or behind their times. For the critic, this means he must be part historian. He will have to reconstruct the historical milieu to understand the intellectual and aesthetic values of the times. He will have to adjust his tastes to those of the period in which the speech appeared. The critic may not appreciate the ponderous Biblical style of the colonial magistrates of 1700, but he must recognize that these speakers were using the language of their time and that it was potentially as effective as our modern conversational style.

The mood and temper of the times may even create the occasion for a speech. Such was the case when General Douglas MacArthur addressed a joint congressional meeting in 1951. The speech was a direct result of his dismissal as commander of military operations in Korea, and his dismissal was a result of the events surrounding the Korean war. No critic could begin to interpret successfully either the immediate audience response or the contents of the speech without being aware of these particular events and of the larger issues of conflict between the military and the U.S. State Department, and between the leaders of the Republicans and the Democrats in Congress and the national administration. All played a part in this famous speech, and the critic would need to make use of them in appraising the speaker, the speech, the audience, and the effects.[9]

At other times, the occasion helps shape the speech in a more formal way. These are the occasions that produce traditional speeches, such as Presidential inaugural addresses, acceptance speeches, speeches of welcome, and speeches of commemoration. Because such occasions are traditional, audiences expect certain

[9]For critical appraisals of the MacArthur speech to Congress, see Frederick W. Haberman, "General MacArthur's Speech: A Symposium of Critical Comment," **The Quarterly Journal of Speech**, XXXVII (October 1951), 321–331; Philip Wylie, "Medievalism and the MacArthurian Legend," **The Quarterly Journal of Speech**, XXXVII (December 1951), 473–478; Karl R. Wallace, "On the Criticism of the MacArthur Speech," **The Quarterly Journal of Speech**, XXXIX (February 1953), 69–74.

Interpreting the speech

"appropriate" subjects and manners of presentation, and the speech must reflect these requirements. The speaker adapts his subject matter accordingly and even uses certain stylized language that is deemed appropriate. The critic, too, takes these strictures into consideration as he analyzes and interprets the speech, for they are all-important in determining the meaning and value of occasional addresses.

An example of a speech that was shaped both by the requirements of the specific occasion and the socio-psychological conditions of the times is Henry Grady's "New South" Speech, delivered in 1886. Marvin G. Bauer analyzes and interprets Grady's rhetorical strategy.

> The temper of the particular period in which a speaker makes his appearance must be kept in mind in order to understand those subtle forces which influence public response. At the time Grady appeared, the movement toward reconciliation between the North and the South was well under way, but there still existed factors that militated against a complete unification, the main one being psychological. . . .
> . . . The yearning for kindly feeling and good will had not yet found adequate expression. And the psychology of the situation demanded that a Southerner carry the message of harmony into the North. From the Northern point of view it was the Southerner who had been the rebel—the troublemaker. Was he now integrating within himself the social, political, and economic patterns of the nation? Lynchings did not indicate such an integration, nor did occasional shootings; and the suppression of the Negro's vote appeared as evidence to the contrary. Could capital flow into the South with safety? Could the Southern politician be trusted? Was the Southerner secretly in his heart harboring bitterness and biding his time for revenge? It is difficult to recreate these forebodings today; but lurking doubts and suspicions still existed in the Northern consciousness as late as 1886. To dispel them, the South must take the initiative in establishing a belief in Southern faith and integrity. . . .
>
> Grady realized the need for the cultivation of this attitude and had that as his purpose when he went to New York City to deliver the address that was to make him famous and inseparably link his name with the idea of **the new south**. . . .
>
> It was given in response to an invitation from the New England Society, organized in 1805 and known for its distinguished membership as well as the long list of outstanding orators who had addressed its meetings. Never before had a Southern man been asked to speak

before it. The invitation to Grady was prompted by a desire for an opinion on the progressive forces at work in the South. The movement toward harmonious relations between the sections had been arrested by a growing political tension that was due to the dissatisfaction of the Republican politicians over the election of Cleveland in 1884, a tension causing considerable uneasiness on the part of businessmen who had invested large sums of money in the South. Much might be gained if some Southern speaker could deliver a message that would tend toward better understanding and cordial relations.

    The situation Grady faced was a difficult one. . . . he therefore devoted almost half of his speech to an introduction in an effort to prepare them for an open-minded reception of his message. He expressed his appreciation of the invitation to speak, made note of "the significance of being the first Southerner to speak at this board," and asked his audience to bring their "full faith in American fairness and frankness to judgment" upon what he had to say. . . . In the humor of his introduction he embedded the indirect suggestion that the stock from which the Southerners had sprung was as important as the ancestry of the New Englanders, and by virtue of the fact Southerners were entitled to as much respect and consideration as Northerners. He quickly utilized his reference to the Cavalier, however, as an opportunity to emphasize the common bond of **tradition** existing between the North and South.

". . . both Puritan and Cavalier were lost in the storm of the first Revolution, and the American citizen, supplanting both and stronger than either, took possession of the Republic bought by their common blood and fashioned to wisdom, and charged himself with teaching men government and establishing the voice of the people as the voice of God. (Applause)"

. . . He had been talking about traditions; it was now in order to talk about heroes. But not Southern heroes or heroes in general. He needed to mention one man in particular, someone not too far back in history to have lost his appeal or too recent for general sentiment to have been built around his name. There was only one logical choice—Abraham Lincoln. Talmage had spoken of "the typical American yet to come," and taking this as a cue, Grady utilized his opportunity to proclaim that the typical American had already come. He gave a glowing tribute to Lincoln, which, according to the **New York Tribune** and other papers, "brought every man to his feet." Grady had met the situation. The crescendo of response grew from "loud and continued applause" to "loud and prolonged cheering." By identifying himself with a sentiment held dear by his audience, he had succeeded in breaking down psychological barriers and stirring his hearers so intensely that from then on they were favorably disposed toward him and his message.[10]

Non-Aristotelian interpretations

The approach of analysis and interpretation of speeches described thus far is essentially a neo-Aristotelian one. It is derived from the theories in Aristotle's **Rhetoric,** and it has been the dominant mode of speech criticism since the 4th century B.C. The Aristotelian critic views a speech as a strategic entity designed to achieve particular results with a specific audience on a specific occasion. He considers that a speech is the result of the application of certain identifiable constituents—invention, arrangement, style, and delivery—and that each one of these canons plays a distinct part in producing the form and content of the speech, and that together they account for the effects of the speech. Further, the Aristotelian critic approaches a speech as a unique artistic effort, the quality of which is determined by the blending of these rhetorical constituents with the needs of the speaker, the subject, the audience, and the occasion.

As was pointed out in Chapter 1, the Aristotelian approach to criticism is appealing because it makes possible a high degree of objectivity; it provides a methodology that can be applied by the critic independent of other critics and yet produce similar conclusions. Thus it offers a kind of scientific-rational approach to the analysis and evaluation of a speech that coincides with the basic assumptions of Aristotle that man is essentially a rational animal in pursuit of truth; and that at its base a speech is primarily a logical construct.

Not everyone would agree with this view of man and his communicative acts. Numerous speeches do not lend themselves readily to Aristotelian interpretations. Consequently, different approaches to speech criticism have been used that produce non-Aristotelian interpretations. Such interpretations are supposed to yield evaluations of speeches uninhibited by the so-called shortcomings of the Aristotelian approach.

Some of these non-Aristotelian approaches to criticism should be

[10]Marvin G. Bauer, "Henry W. Grady," in **A History and Criticism of American Public Address,** Vol. I, ed. W. N. Brigance (New York: McGraw-Hill, 1943), pp. 387–391. Used by permission of McGraw-Hill Book Co.

discussed so that their interpretations may be contrasted with Aristotelian interpretations. These are Edwin Black's exhortative-argumentative approach, Kenneth Burke's dramatistic approach, I. A. Richards' language-meaning approach, and Alfred Korzybski's language-reality approach.

Black's exhortative-argumentative criticism. Edwin Black, after studying Aristotelian criticism, has found it wanting. He says:

> ... The neo-Aristotelians ignore the impact of the discourse on rhetorical conventions, its capacity for disposing an audience to expect certain ways of arguing and certain kinds of justifications in later discourses that they encounter, even on different subjects. Similarly, the neo-Aristotelian critics do not account for the influence of the discourse on its author: the future commitments it makes for him, rhetorically and ideologically; the choices it closes to him, rhetorically and ideologically; the public image it portrays to which he must adjust.[11]

He feels that Aristotelian criticism is much too restrictive; it places too much emphasis on the immediate audience and the immediate effects of a speech; it inhibits the critic in his search for the far-reaching social and ethical implications of a speech.

Further, Black sees the Aristotelian approach as unrealistic. He believes that audiences do not necessarily operate logically in arriving at their beliefs; rather, it is emotionalism that produces belief. Black claims that:

> So long as the doctrines of Aristotelianism are applied to rational discourses addressed to judicious audiences, they are useful; but they cannot be extended beyond this scope without misapplication. There is no outrage to reason we can imagine that has not ample historical precedent. In consequence, the assumption of rational behavior that lies behind the enthymeme renders that formulation inapplicable to numberless rhetorical transactions.[12]

To offset Aristotelian restrictions and to find a more realistic approach to criticism, Black has established a scale of rhetorical transactions, i.e., speech strategies, situations, and effects, that lays out human communications from one extreme to the other. He has looked for "congregations of discourse," places on the scale where

---
[11]Edwin Black, **Rhetorical Criticism** (New York: Macmillan, 1965), pp. 34–35. Reprinted with permission of the publisher.
[12]**Ibid.**, pp. 127–128.

discourses pile up, indicating which are the most widely used rhetorical transactions. These locations provide an operational description of the rhetorical transactions in which men most frequently participate. Black suggests that at each one of these points, a hierarchy of best to worst transactions could be established and used to measure comparably any rhetorical discourse belonging at that point.

Black has found two such points of congregation on his scale of rhetorical transactions; one he labels **exhortative,** the other **argumentative.** He conceives of exhortative discourse as basically different in genre from any described in Aristotle's rhetoric.

> ... Such a genre of discourse is that in which the evocation of an emotional response in the audience induces belief in the situation to which the emotion is appropriate. In this genre, a strong emotional experience does not follow the acceptance of a belief, or even accompany it; it precedes it. Emotion can be said to produce belief, instead of the reverse.[13]

Exhortative discourse, for Black, covers all those speeches that depend for their effect on the stirring of emotional responses in the audience rather than on the laying out of logical arguments.

The characteristic strategies or exhortative discourse that Black would have the critic look for are, "extensive use of concrete description," and "the frequent use of **is** or **will be** or **should** or **should be.**" He finds that appropriate concrete language is more likely to produce a strong effective response than is abstract language, and that claims about what **is** or what **will be** carry greater emotional weight than the advocacy of what **ought to be.** When these two strategies are successfully employed, the auditor finds his attention captured and his emotions aroused to the point that he "must account for his own feelings to himself. This self-accounting, urged by the exhorter, involves the acceptance of a conviction."[14]

The exhortative speech uses language and emotion to produce conviction by capitalizing on the human proclivity to validate feelings by accepting appropriate beliefs. Using Black's method, the rhetorical critic analyzes and interprets exhortative speeches by determining the potential of the emotion produced to achieve the

---
[13]Ibid., p. 138.
[14]Ibid., p. 145.

desired belief. The critic considers the appropriateness of the language and the emotion to the psychological condition of the audience; the surrounding circumstances; and the legitimacy of the belief desired.

Black provides an example of this type of criticism in his appraisal of the "Coatesville Address" by John Jay Chapman. The speech commemorating the first anniversary of a brutal lynching of a Negro in Coatesville, Pennsylvania, was delivered to an audience of three persons on Sunday, August 18, 1912. The following are excerpts from Black's criticism of this little-known address:

> The verdict of neo-Aristotelianism on this speech would have been negative. It did not fetch results. . . .
>
> . . . The speech had virtually no immediate audience anyhow, and why bother with a soliloquy that was overheard by three people? And yet, as Edmund Wilson has commented, the speech is "strange and moving."
>
> Moving it is, moving enough so that the bare calculation of its immediate effects is insufficient to account for it, moving enough so that the contemporary reader cannot feel its power as having been spent on that audience of three. The speech is not a cold marble monument. It lives. But to see its life, we must find its proper context.
>
> The context of the Coatesville Address is not the vacant grocery store of 1912. Rather, the discourse must be understood as joining the dialogue participated in by Jefferson, Tocqueville, Lincoln, Melville, Henry Adams, Samuel Clemens, Santayana, and Faulkner—a dialogue on the moral dimension of the American experience. The Coatesville Address is a particularly interesting statement in the dialogue because it is one of the very few of this century that is not cast in the form of fiction. . . .
>
> Our warrant for taking the context of the Coatesville Address so broadly is suggested by Chapman himself. The first two paragraphs insistently demand that his auditors focus, not on Coatesville, but on the country. His very first idea is that "our whole people are involved in the guilt." From there he talks of "American citizens . . . of the American heart and of the American nature." Later he makes it explicit: ". . . this great wickedness that happened in Coatesville is not the wickedness of Coatesville nor of today. It is the wickedness of all America and of three hundred years. . . ."
>
> So much for context. Next we must consider what the speech actually says. It is, most obviously, an interpretation of an event. . . .

> Chapman . . . shapes a perception of the lynching that moderates outrage with detachment, moderates it, in fact, so extensively that it is substantively transformed and becomes a reaction for which we have no precise word in English. We do not need a word so long as we have Chapman's speech, for it enables us to experience the reaction. We are his audience.
>
> Chapman would have us perceive the event as a scene in a morality play. The play itself is the history of this country, seen as the death-through-sin and the potential rebirth-through-purification of a whole people. The issues of crime and punishment, of blame and defense, would not shape the auditor's response, just as they do not shape it in a tragic drama. The lynching is seen as a ritual murder, and the appropriate response to it is a religious experience. We are able, through this response, to view the lynching unequivocally as a crime, and yet we do not hate the criminals, for we feel ourselves to be responsible. The net practical effect of the speech on the thoroughly attentive auditor is to make him incapable of lynching—incapable because, instead of being aware of a specific and singular case, he has become aware of the moral nature of lynching. He has, in sum, not simply a moral reaction, but a moral insight.[15]

The second congregation of discourses on Black's scale of rhetorical transactions is labeled "the genre of argumentation." Defining argumentation, he says: "It is not only relatively reasonable discourse, soliciting an assent less intense than, say, exhortation, and more intense than, say, advice-giving, but it is also discourse that occurs in a situation of controversy."[16] It is the dimension of controversy that Black finds most significant in analyzing and interpreting the argumentative genre.

> The fact the critic of argumentation must take into account is that there are always a protagonist and antagonist in the argumentative situation. The rhetor has [an] active opponent; one who attacks, and who strategically counters the rhetor's own strategies. . . . The rhetor then is compelled to produce discourse that can overcome an active opposition and, simultaneously, contribute to the attractiveness and credibility of the rhetor's ideas. How well or ill the rhetor performs this dual task is an important criterion to the rhetorical critic of argumentation.[17]

[15]Ibid., p. 82–88. To do justice to this unique, interesting interpretation the reader should consider it in its entirety.
[16]Ibid., p. 149.
[17]Ibid., p. 150.

To Black, argument is on-going: it may never reach resolution, as in the argument over the relationship of the individual to the state; or it may find resolution only in conflict, such as in our own Civil War. Thus, Black would want the critic to examine argument as a historic **process** and evaluate argumentative discourses for their contribution to this process, rather than as isolated events in which speakers "win" arguments with rhetorical strategies.

Black would require the critic to understand the argumentative function as he sees it. The critic should recognize that all persons hold "clusters of opinion" with which they form their own "synthetic universes." That is, people have sets of beliefs that they put together to form a world that is compatible with these beliefs. However, these clusters of opinion are not always compatible, such as occurs when a person believes that war is evil but believes also that his country ought to fight to keep its colonial possessions. Or when, as times change, old clusters of opinion conflict with newly acquired beliefs. It is the presence of incompatibilities that leads to controversy in which various beliefs compete with one another, which in turn produces discourses designed to resolve these difficulties.

For a speaker to be successful in an argumentative discourse, he must not only gain the acceptance of a belief, he must gain allegiance to a whole series of beliefs that can be made compatible with the clusters of opinion held by his hearers. Black calls this **argumentative synthesis:** a process in which the speaker persuades the audience to accept certain beliefs while at the same time dissuading them from other beliefs that are incompatible with the desired beliefs. In so doing, the speaker provides hearers with a satisfactory synthetic universe. It is this argumentative synthesis that is the key to interpretation of Black's genre of argumentation.

Black demonstrates this approach in analyzing and interpreting the Lincoln-Douglas debates and Lincoln's Second Inaugural Address. Of the latter he says:

> Lincoln's Second Inaugural address is an interesting specimen to consider with regard to argumentative synthesis because it is an exception to the rule of length. It is a brief speech by the standards of Lincoln's time, too brief, it would seem, to create a universe of discourse. Yet it discloses a cluster of opinions which was certainly alien to the auditors of 1865 in its detachment from chauvinism, its historical perspective, and its pervasive sense of tragedy. Add to the list

the tone of compassion in the speech and its rejection of retributive justice, and a universe begins to take shape. It was a universe of discourse that few of Lincoln's auditors ever finally inhabited, but that does not deter us, a century later, from finding the speech highly meritorious. It is true that the policies of reconstruction that followed Lincoln's death can be regarded as evidence that his views failed to take hold, hence that he was a rhetorical failure. But we must equally bear in mind that he was twice elected to the presidency, and he is now an incomparable hero. The rhetorical triumphs are more striking than the rhetorical failures. These triumphs, and especially the increasing enhancement of his reputation after his death, can be illuminated by reference to argumentative synthesis. Lincoln created a coherent universe in which major public issues were arranged in an hierarchy of order and thus were brought under linguistic control. His reputation has been enhanced as his universe of discourse is clarified through the exegesis of his speeches and writings. Such clarification does take time, and that may be one reason for our thinking better of Lincoln's speeches than did many of his contemporaries. In any event, although the strategy of argumentative synthesis does require a certain quantitative latitude for its perfection, it can serve as a critical instrument for single speeches.[18]

In concluding his study of the genre of argumentation, Black suggests that the rhetorical critic consider this type of speech as part of a historic process of argument, evaluating the speech as it is related to its antecedents and its consequences. In this way, the critic copes with the entire sweep of argumentative process, rather than with an isolated event.

Burke's dramatistic criticism. The approach to rhetorical criticism made popular by Kenneth Burke in his various works since 1931 is known as a **dramatistic** one, so named because Burke views man as an actor, acting out his purpose on a life stage. Because he is a symbol-using animal, man's acts are mostly verbal. Because he is a socio-psychological animal, the part a man plays in this drama is determined by his motives. This dramatistic approach "invites one to consider the matter of motives in a perspective that, being developed from the analysis of drama, treats language and thought primarily as modes of action."[19] Thus, all criticism, if it is to be

[18]**Ibid.**, p. 172.
[19]Kenneth Burke, **A Grammar of Motives** (New York: Prentice-Hall, 1945), p. xxii.

meaningful, must interpret the verbal inducements of men as motivated acts in this social drama. It is through language that man induces cooperation and understanding, and therefore action, in an otherwise divisive world. Burke claims that viewing language in this manner would bring within the scope of rhetoric any and all symbolic resources that function to promote social cohesion, and all symbolic resources that induce attitude or action.

To provide a system by which one can analyze these rhetorical functions Burke has established a dramatic pentad:

> Act, Scene, Agent, Agency, Purpose. In a rounded statement about motives you must have some work that names the **act** (names what took place, in thought and deed), and another that names the **scene** (the background of the act, the situation in which it occurred); also, you must indicate what person or kind of person (agent) performed the act, what means or instrument he used (agency), and the **purpose**. Men may violently disagree about the purposes behind a given act, or about the character of the person who did it, or how he did it, or in what kind of situation he acted; or they may even insist upon totally different words to name the act itself. But be that as it may, any complete statement about motives will offer **some kind** of answers to these five questions: what was done (act), when or where it was done (scene), who did it (agent), how he did it (agency), and why (purpose).[20]

According to Burke, the speech critic uses this construct for speech analysis by determining what was said (act), under what circumstances (scene), by whom (agent), using what linguistic structures and strategies (agency), to accomplish what end (purpose).

This analysis differs from the traditional Aristotelian analysis of speaker, speech, audience, and occasion because it stresses how language functions in producing the interrelatedness of these five items, instead of viewing language as an overlaid function (style) on the rational design (invention and arrangement) of a speech. Marie Hochmuth Nichols, in describing how Burke would analyze and interpret a speech, says:

> . . . he will search a text for the coordinates of what goes with what and with what follows what in the hope of discovering the recurrent strategies of identification. By constantly asking the question: How is language acting to obtain its ends? he believes that one can find out something about the nature of meaning, motive, human relations in

[20]Ibid., p. xv.

general. By what agent, using what agency, in what scene, for what purpose is language acting to encompass the situation? Language-using of any kind is a response to a situation which arises—and is not only a response, but a strategic response, a stylized response.[21]

There are several key terms in the Burkean lexicon; the two most important for the speech critic are **identification** and **strategies.** Of the first term, Burke states: "The key term for the old rhetoric was 'persuasion' and its stress was upon deliberate design. The key term for the 'new' rhetoric would be **'identification,'** which can include a partially 'unconscious' factor in appeal."[22] Identification is the process of overcoming those things that divide men by providing them with concepts, images, ideas, and attitudes that allow them to become substantially one (consubstantial, to use Burke's term) with other persons, groups, or institutions. Persuasion takes place when something is done that establishes identification through **act, agent** and **scene,** which makes the receiver consubstantial with the **purpose.** The agency would be the **strategies** employed to bring about this identification.

Burke believes that people bring attitudes to every situation in which they are a part and that they try to modify situations to fit their existing attitudes. The methods people use to bring about these modifications he calls their strategies. Burke claims that, "One seeks to 'direct the larger movements and operations' in one's campaign of living. One 'maneuvers,' and the maneuvering is an 'art.' Are not the final results one's 'strategy'?"[23] Strategies then combine both attitude and method. The speaker seeks to identify audience attitudes in a situation with his own. His attitude toward this act (situation) determines the strategies he will use with the audience.

The task for the rhetorical critic, using Burkean criticism, is to analyze the strategies in the speech act and to interpret how language is acting to obtain desired ends. He needs to answer questions about why the speaker spoke as he did, and how the language

---

[21]Marie Hochmuth Nichols, **Rhetoric and Criticism** (Baton Rouge: Louisiana State University Press, 1963), p. 91.
[22]Kenneth Burke, "Rhetoric—Old and New," **The Journal of General Education,** V (April 1951), 203.
[23]Kenneth Burke, **The Philosophy of Literary Form** (Baton Rouge: Louisiana State University Press, 1941) p. 297.

symbols functioned to produce or reduce identification. To do this successfully, the critic has to know the social scene and be cognizant of the socio-psychological symbols operating.

Kenneth Burke himself provides us with an example of Burkean critical analysis and interpretation. He selects as his case Hitler's **Mein Kampf,** which he considers a rhetorical (persuasive) genre— a highly successful one. The following is an excerpt from his detailed criticism of this work:

> Every movement that would recruit its followers from among many discordant and divergent bands, must have some spot towards which all roads lead. Each man may get there in his own way, but it must be the one unifying center of reference for all. Hitler considered this matter carefully, and decided that this center must be not merely a centralizing hub of **ideas,** but a mecca geographically located, towards which all eyes could turn at the appointed hours of prayer (or, in this case, the appointed hours of prayer-in-reverse, the hours of vituperation). So he selected Munich, as the **materialization** of his unifying panacea. As he puts it:
>
> "The geo-political importance of a center of a movement cannot be overrated. Only the presence of such a center and of a place, bathed in the magic of a Mecca or a Rome, can at length give a movement that force which is rooted in the inner unity and in the recognition of a hand that represents this unity."
>
> If a movement must have its Rome, it must also have its devil. For as Russell pointed out years ago, an important ingredient of unity in the Middle Ages (an ingredient that long did its unifying work despite the many factors driving toward disunity) was the symbol of a **common enemy,** the Prince of Evil himself. Men who can unite on nothing else can unite on the basis of a foe shared by all. Hitler himself states the case very succinctly:
>
> "As a whole, and at all times, the efficiency of the truly national leader consists primarily in preventing the division of the attention of a people, and always in concentrating it on a single enemy. The more uniformly the fighting will of a people is put into action, the greater will be the magnetic force of the movement and the more powerful the impetus of the blow. It is part of the genius of a great leader to make adversaries of different fields appear as always belonging to one category only, because to weak and unstable characters the knowledge that there are various enemies will lead only too easily to incipient doubts as to their own cause.
>
> "As soon as the wavering masses find themselves confronted with

too many enemies, objectivity at once steps in, and the question is raised whether actually all the others are wrong and their own nation or their own movement alone is right.

"Also with this comes the first paralysis of their own strength. Therefore, a number of essentially different enemies must always be regarded as one in such a way that in the opinion of the mass of one's own adherents the war is being waged against one enemy alone. This strengthens the belief in one's own cause and increases one's bitterness against the attacker."

As everyone knows, this policy was exemplified in his selection of an "international" devil, the "international Jew" (the Prince was international, universal, "catholic"). The **materialization** of a religious pattern is, I think, one terrifically effective weapon of propaganda in a period where religion has been progressively weakened by many centuries of capitalist materialism. . . .[24]

Richard's language-meaning criticism. Like Kenneth Burke, I. A. Richards is concerned with language functions, but his concern is at once more narrow and more penetrating. Richards' rhetoric is a "philosophic inquiry into how words work in discourse"[25] and a method of determining the meaning of statements in all forms of discourse. He urges that, "Rhetoric . . . should be a study of misunderstanding and its remedies. We struggle all our days with misunderstandings, and no apology is required for any study which can prevent or remove them."[26] His chief concern is with **how words mean**. He puts his concern in the form of a question:

> . . . What is the connection between the mind and the world by which events in the mind mean other events in the world? Or, How does a thought come to be "of" whatever it is that it is a thought "of?" or "What is the relation between a thing and its name?"[27]

The "old rhetoric" (Richards' term for rhetorical theory from Aristotle to Whately), he claims, was much too concerned with strategies and dodges for winning arguments. It was based on the "combative impulse," and it produced a method of winning assent through prose discourse, i.e., the means of persuasion. To Richards, this rhetoric of persuasion is "an exploitation of a systematic set of misunderstandings for war-like purposes." Richards' new rhetoric con-

[24]**Ibid.**, pp. 192–194. Reprinted by permission of the author.
[25]**The Philosophy of Rhetoric**, p. 8.
[26]**Ibid.**, p. 3.
[27]**Ibid.**, p. 28.

centrates on the fundamental laws of the use of language and uses them to minister to understanding and prevent misunderstanding.

Richards rejects the traditional canons of rhetoric as artificial divisions of thought and language that have never been proven to exist. He claims that:

> ... we **can** only "collect the whole sum and tenor of the discourse" from the words, we cannot "lay aside the words"; ... considering "the bare notions themselves." ... Indeed an idea, or a notion, like the physicists' ultimate particles and rays, is only known by what it does. Apart from its dress or other signs it is not identifiable.[28]

Beginning with identifiable signs—words—Richards concentrates on the functions of language rather than theoretical thought processes. He discusses abstraction, definition, metaphor, and thought-word-thing relationships. Always, his concern is with how these functions produce meaning. He warns:

> ... we must study with and through words. ... Whatever we may be studying we do so only through the growth of our meanings. To realize this turns some parts of this attempted direct study of the modes of growth and interaction between meanings, which might otherwise seem a niggling philosophic juggle with distinctions, into a business of great practical importance.[29]

Of those rhetorics in the past that have viewed communication as primarily a stylistic problem (e.g., Longinus, **On the Sublime**; Talaeus, **Rhetorica**), Richards claims that they did little more than provide labels—imagery, figures, schemes, tropes, irony—and commonsense admonitions—be clear, be vivid, be perspicuous. He faults them for failing to inquire into the whole action of words, for limiting their concern to the large-scale disposals of meaning. To overcome the shortcomings of these older language approaches Richards would:

> ... shift the focus of our analysis and attempt a deeper and more minute grasp and try to take account of the structures of the smallest discussable units of meaning and the ways in which these vary as they are put with other units.[30]

For the speech critic, the Richards language-meaning approach

[28] Ibid., p. 5.
[29] Ibid., p. 19.
[30] Ibid., pp. 9–10.

requires that he understand language functions—abstraction, definition, metaphor, etc.—and that he analyze the units of meaning as they exist in a particular discourse. To determine meaning, Richards would have the critic regard the words spoken from four points of view: (1) sense, (2) feeling, (3) tone, and (4) intention. A speaker directs the hearer's thoughts to some items for consideration (sense); the speaker has attitudes or feelings toward these items that are expressed in the words used (feeling); furthermore, the speaker has an attitude toward his listener, the meaning of which is found in the statements chosen (tone); finally, the speaker has an aim, conscious or unconscious, which he is promoting, adding another meaning that is reflected in all the statements of a given discourse (intention). The critic's task is to analyze the discourse for its total meaning—this includes an analysis of the hearers from each of these four points of view to determine what meanings they would give to the speaker's words.

To evaluate a communication, Richards would have the critic assess all its meaning units for their contribution to creating understanding and lessening misunderstanding. The critic judges the speech by its efficacy in promoting comprehension of meaning.[31]

Korzybski's language-reality criticism. Alfred Korzybski, founder of the General Semantics Movement, sought a new linguistic method consistent with our scientific age. He began by rejecting Aristotelian modes of thought and language as primitive and misleading. To him, Aristotle's logic was based upon false assumptions about the factual world; it tried to divide a dynamic, ever-changing world into fixed categories, in which the truth of things and events could be known by relating them to their correct categories. These false assumptions led to language forms that treated multifaceted, ever-evolving realities as though they were static entities that could be identified and labeled (e.g., That object is a tree. That boy is bad.), and that created fictitious entities, such as "communist," "scholar," "gangster," that do not have any factual counterpart in the world of reality (i.e., there is only man [1] in situation [1] and neither he nor the situation remains fixed).

---

[31] Needless to say, in these few paragraphs we have not done justice to I. A. Richards' great contributions to the study of language. The reader is referred to his **The Philosophy of Rhetoric** and **Practical Criticism** (New York: Harcourt, Brace, 1954), and the monumental **The Meaning of Meaning**, written with C. K. Ogden (London: Routledge & Kegan Paul, 1923).

The great sin of the Aristotelian approach, according to Korzybski, is that it blurs the line between the factual world and the verbal world. As a result, men are forever thinking that their verbal statements are complete and accurate descriptions of the real world, and they often act as though the **word is the object**. These semantic reactions—reactions to words instead of things—block man's evaluative functions, making him incapable of adjusting to the world of reality, in turn leading to personal and social maladjustments. To overcome these linguistic blocks, Korzybski would have man develop a new "organism-as-a-whole" or nonelementalistic language form that corresponds to the factual structures of the nonverbal world. Korzybski believes that:

> The **non-el** [nonelementalistic] principle formulates a structural character inherently found in the structure of the world, ourselves, and our nervous systems on all levels; the knowledge and application of which is unconditionally necessary for adjustment at all levels, and therefore, in humans, for sanity.[32]

Korzybski would build scientifically new language forms whose structure corresponds to the structure found experimentally in nature. These new language forms would produce semantic reactions that were true to reality, free of the deceptive qualities of the old language forms. These results would be assured because:

> . . . As "knowledge," "understanding," and such functions are **solely** relational, and, therefore, structural, the unconditional and inherent condition for adjustment on all human levels depends on building languages of similar structure to the experimental facts. Once this is accomplished, all the former desirably semantic consequences will follow automatically.[33]

Space does not permit a discussion of the many forms and principles of a General Semantics rhetoric. For an understanding of the "non-el" principle, multi-ordinal relations, the intensional-extensional principle, the ladder of abstraction, non-allness, non-isness, and indexing, the reader is referred to Korzybski's **Science and Sanity** and its popularized versions: S. I. Hayakawa, **Language in Thought and Action;** Irving J. Lee, **Language Habits in Human**

---

[32]Alfred Korzybski, **Science and Sanity**, 3rd ed., rev. (Lakeville, Conn.: The International Non-Aristotelian Library, 1948), p. 130.
[33]**Ibid.**

Affairs; and Wendell Johnson, **People in Quandaries.** All espouse a rhetoric that focuses on the **relationships of words to facts,** and that places the burden on the speaker of maintaining a constant vigil over his verbalizations, making certain that his "word-maps" fit the "fact-territory" so that his own and his hearer's reactions will be adequately adjusted to reality.

Although there is not yet a body of criticism that uses the General Semantics approach exclusively, Irving Lee has explained the method of analysis to be used by the General Semanticist critic. The critic uses "a methodology which reveals the unnoticed nuances and subtleties of inaccuracy and misevaluation."[34] In analyzing a speech he determines:

> ... Does it make sense? Does the speech properly evaluate whatever the words are intended to represent? How does what is said correspond to what can be found in life? ... [The critic] keeps constantly and uppermost the connections between two levels: the verbal and the non-verbal, the worlds of the speakable and the unspeakable. He seeks to check the language at every point for the relationship it has to the discoverable facts of life.[35]

To evaluate a speech, Lee recommends that the critic judge:

> ... the "good sense" of the speech ... the nicety with which the speaker discriminates ... the degree with which we can, with security, rely on his evaluations. ... If his [the speaker's] language use is cluttered up with identifications, objectifications, distortions, oversimplifications—then for our survival, those evidences of immaturity and unintelligence must be revealed.[36]

It has been possible to touch only lightly upon the critical approaches of Black, Burke, Richards, and Korzybski. Nevertheless, if this brief presentation has served to indicate that rhetorical criticism is not a rigid or static art, but a dynamic and growing one involving many schools of thought, it has served a useful purpose. We should remember that the interpretations and evaluations a critic makes of a speech are dependent, in large part, upon which theory of rhetoric he upholds and the critical methodology he ap-

---

[34]Irving J. Lee, "Four Ways of Looking At a Speech," **The Quarterly Journal of Speech,** XXVIII (April 1942), 153.
[35]Ibid., p. 154.
[36]Ibid., p. 155.

plies. Consequently, there may be several valid interpretations of a speech. The value of these interpretations will depend on how thoroughly the critic has mastered his art and how well grounded it is in a cohesive rhetorical theory. It is not a matter of having **the one** correct approach to speech criticism so much as having a well-developed and consistent philosophy of rhetoric and criticism.

FIVE

Evaluating the speech

The end sought in criticism is a **judgment** of the work under consideration. Without final evaluation, a rhetorical critique is incomplete. Accurate description and analysis of a speech may tell us what went on and why, and careful interpretation may reveal the meaning of the constituents of the speech; but, without an evaluation of the speaker's intent, the method of the speech, and the effects, we would have only synthetic criticism. We might comprehend the speech in all its intricacies, but not know its artistic quality nor its social worth. We might be aware of the speaker's choices, but not know how rhetorically sound they were. We might know the speech effects, but not know if they were desirable. To repeat, a critique is not complete until the critic gives his judgment.

One of the justifications of criticism is that through the judicious appraisal of speeches both the practice of speech-making and the art of rhetoric are continually re-evaluated. Without judgments of the rhetorical qualities of a speech, the critic adds little to the knowledge of the art of discourse. The critic must be able to determine whether the speech has contributed to both the elevation of man and the furthering of effective communication. A significant criticism is one in which the critic has rendered a judgment and has placed the speech in the unending stream of suasive discourse. A critique that only reveals the speech may be useful to the study of rhetoric, but every critique that reveals **and** evaluates advances the art of rhetoric.

This final chapter will cover the three types of judgment the critic makes in evaluating a speech. He must judge: (1) the effects of the speech—both the potential effects of the written speech, and the discernible effects of the delivered speech; (2) the quality of the speech—its creative merits as a literary form; (3) the worth of the speech—its contributions to social values and its consequences in society. The purpose of this chapter is to provide the critic with guidelines for the successful performance of the last step in the critical process—evaluation. Previous chapters have reviewed the methods of describing, analyzing, and interpreting speeches. Each of those processes is a stepping stone to the final task of the critic: the making of a judicious evaluation of the speech.

Problems of evaluation

Making a judicious evaluation requires that the critic be aware of the intricacies of human communication and cognizant that he can never know everything about the communicative situation. An untrained critic is quick to render an impressionistic judgment because he is unaware of all the variables that are operative. The trained critic knows that many factors account for the effects of a speech and that making an evaluation of them places a great burden on him. The trained critic establishes the connection between his judgments and the effects of the speech; he defends his conclusions; he proves that his assessments are reasonable.

The major problem the critic faces in making this reasoned evaluation is that of establishing both standards of judgment and a method that will provide application of standards to the work in question. Chapter 2 discussed disagreements over standards used in judging a speech. It was suggested that no one of the standards of truth, motive, or results alone provides the critic with one suitable standard. Rather, the standard of artistic excellence that includes logic, intent, and response is most in keeping with the view of rhetoric as the art of adaptation and adjustment. The adoption of the artistic standard, however, still leaves the critic with the problem of determining what constitutes artistic quality and worth. Does one judge the artistic excellence of a speech by how well and to what end the speaker utilized all the available means of persuasion? If so, how does one determine the most effective and desirable uses of this available means of persuasion?

Standards of judgment. Only through knowing what constitutes the best communicative performance, as well as knowing what other critics have established as standards of judgment, can one answer these questions. The knowledge can be acquired through study of historical speeches and critiques; through understanding the rhetorical principles derived from past observations and criticisms; and through application of the scientific findings of psychologists and sociologists about behavioral responses to verbal stimuli. To judge a speech by the artistic standard, the critic should be able to compare the speech with what has been achieved in past discourses and what current knowledge of communication theory suggests that an ideal discourse ought to achieve.

In making such appraisals, the critic must avoid the pitfall of assuming that each speech performance is its own end, unique and incomparable to any past performance. At the same time, he must not make judgments based solely on the comparison of one performance with a previous one, no matter how similar the two circumstances. In the first instance, the critic would be left with no basis for comparison, and in the second one, he would have to deny that any speech could exceed the best past performance. In arriving at a standard of artistic quality and worth, the critic must know what a rhetorical performance **ought to do** as well as **what it is capable of doing.** To know what a speech is capable of doing, he must, based upon his understanding of rhetorical theory, formulate his own concepts of what would be the ideal speech, i.e., what he considers the wisest and most ethical uses of rhetoric.

Methods of judgment. Given a standard by which to appraise speeches, the critic faces the task of applying that standard and arriving at a judgment. The **method** that he uses to do this will influence his evaluation. Does he start with the speaker and his purpose and then determine how close the speaker came to achieving his end? Or does he look at the speech itself to determine how perfect it is rhetorically, no matter what the effects? Or does he begin with the social milieu and determine how worthy the speech was in promoting those truths most highly valued in the society? Depending on the method used, critics derive different judgments, even when they use the same standards.

The method used in arriving at a judgment will depend upon assumptions made about the place and function of rhetoric in our society. If the critic sees rhetoric as a means to personal power—a means by which to influence and control others—then he looks at the speaker and the audience to see how artfully the speaker went about his task of effecting social control. He will ask what the speaker achieved by his artistry and what could he have achieved had he used the principles of the art of rhetoric to their fullest? If he, the critic, sees rhetoric as one of the forms of the literary genre, a genre that includes poetics and dramatics and that appeals to the reason and imagination of man through the logical and aesthetic application of language symbols, then he will look at the speech to determine how eloquent it is. As a critic, he will look at the artistic qualities of the arguments and language no matter who the speaker or who the listener. If the critic sees rhetoric as a force that shapes the culture and sets before society that which is most valuable in man's continuing quest for enlightenment and achievement of the good life, then he will look for the ideas and insights contained in the speech for their furtherance of the cause of humanity, no matter how ineloquently they may have been stated.

Using the first method, the critic will praise those speeches that bring the best men to power and enable them to lead others effectively. Using the second, he will esteem most highly those speeches that contain statements of permanence and beauty, appealing to all men for all time. Using the third method, he will value most those speeches that contribute to the actualization of social values.

It is not easy to make each of these methods of evaluation distinct from the other two. Though critics tend to lean toward one or another of the methods depending on their philosophy, all three methods overlap. For example, a speaker judged to have effectively exercised great personal power may have acquired this, in part, because of the eloquent language of his speeches. The author believes that all three of these methods of evaluation are useful. The critic should know each of them because together they will help him evaluate the speech in all of its ramifications. That he may choose to consider one more important than another is his right.

The effects of the speech

Speaking seeks a response. The speaker wishes to control the behavior of his auditors; he wants both an immediate and long-range attitude change. He is not likely to be satisfied with his communication unless he obtains his desired response. The same holds true for the audience. The audience desires understandings, satisfactions, and so forth, and it responds to the speech in various ways, depending on how well the speech meets audience needs. Thus, effects are a concomitant of rhetorical discourse; one cannot exist without the other. It follows then that the critic should be concerned with effects and with the means employed by the speaker to produce effects consistent with his intent and audience needs.

Determining the effects of a speech is not a simple matter, as was pointed out in Chapter 2. There may be little or no discernible immediate audience response, yet the speech may produce strong delayed response. Another speech may produce an immediate, overt audience response, with little or no delayed reaction. Moreover, a speech may be warmly received by its immediate audience, yet create unfavorable reactions in the larger audience that reads the speech in the papers the next day. A case in point is Barry M. Goldwater's acceptance address after his nomination as the Republican Presidential candidate in 1964.

Though the responses of the audience may be indefinable, and the critic unsure of cumulative effects, he must, nevertheless, evaluate the effects of the speech. To do this, he judges its **potential** effect, i.e., what it ought to be able to effect rhetorically. Even where he does have sure evidence of the extrinsic effects of a speech, the critic will need to examine the speech internally for causal relationships to know whether or not the effects produced were commensurate with the rhetorical methods employed.

Analysis and interpretation of a speech gives the critic a fairly clear picture of the speaker's intent and his specific purpose (see Chapters 2 and 3). With this knowledge, the critic can begin an evaluation of the potential or intrinsic effects of the speech. He must assume that speeches do produce results and that there is a connection between those results and the speaker's purpose even though it is not always completely clear how those results are determined. If, for example, the speaker's intent is to mislead or misinform his audience, then it must be assumed that it is possible for the speaker to achieve this. The effect would be that of making the audience less able to develop insight and understanding into the subject or problem at hand. Given this analysis and interpretation of a speech, the critic would have to evaluate the needs of the speaker and the audience and make his judgment of the effects accordingly.

Occasionally, study of a speech reveals that the speaker intended to promote hysteria or create confusion, which would, in turn, make it more difficult for his hearers to reach rational conclusions. No matter how skillfully the speech might be developed or what the ultimate aims of the speaker were, the critic must judge the speaker and speech according to the effects likely to be produced should the speaker succeed in his purpose. One may find examples of this in the recent speeches of some of the more demagogic Southern segregationists. Their speeches may include eloquent appeals for states' rights and local autonomy, but their purpose may well be to create confusion, in the minds of Southerners and Northerners alike, on the issues of civil rights. The critic must make his judgment of such speeches in light of the potential effects on both listener and speaker.

It is obvious what judgment the critic should make when the speaker's purpose is clearly base and deceitful, but what of the effects of speeches in which it is the speaker's intent to "play it safe" or to build his own image without offending anybody? What are the effects of speeches by politicians who want to be elected but who do not want to commit themselves to positions on issues; who want to avoid all controversy? The critic must judge if the potential effects are valuable rhetorically. Do they enhance the prestige and power of the speaker, do they give guidance to the audience, do they produce rational thought and good conduct, do they enable speaker and hearer to understand one another better? If speaking is fundamentally a response-getting activity, then the value of the intended response is related to all the effects that accrue from the speech and is necessarily part of the critic's evaluation.

Judging the speaker's purpose is only part of the evaluation of the intrinsic or potential effects of a speech. The speaker may have good intentions and establish a purpose well suited to the needs of his hearers and to the demands of the problem, and yet he may produce results that are hardly in keeping with his high purpose. No matter what the purpose, the effects of a speech are determined in

Evaluating the speech

large measure by the rhetorical means employed. Some speeches of fine purpose produce negative effects because the speaker fails to employ appropriate arguments, to arouse the audience to some acceptable goal with suitable motivation, or to use language that is clear and understandable. In other speeches, the speaker has high aims but uses doubtful means to achieve those ends. In all these cases, the critic must look at the rhetorical means employed, the issues selected, the facts presented and omitted, the personal and emotional appeals employed and the language used, and determine the effects, both immediate and long range. The critic must evaluate the means the speaker uses to achieve his end and the potential effects produced by such means. He must judge whether or not these are the best means available and the most desirable effects.

Besides the intrinsic or potential effects of a speech, the **actual** effects of the speech on its auditors, both immediate and removed, must be evaluated.

Determining the specific effects of a communication on its many audiences is a problem both rhetoricians and behavioral scientists have to consider. Where an immediate overt response (such as a vote) is called for, the effect of a speech may be determined with some degree of accuracy. But most speeches seek changes in attitudes or points of view, and the responses to these goals are difficult to determine. One method used is to collect various commentaries on the speech to see what patterns of response are indicated. Thus, a critic will check newspaper editorials and other sources of commentary to determine what the general response has been to, let us say, for example, a President's State of the Union Address. He will then evaluate this response by judging it against the best possible response the speaker could have obtained under the circumstances.

Another method of determining the effects of a speech for purposes of evaluation is to look at the speech historically for possible causation between the communication and later events. President John F. Kennedy delivered a speech in favor of a nuclear-test-ban treaty in August 1963; one month later, the Senate voted in favor of such a test ban. The critic might say that these effects were produced in part by the speech and then proceed to judge the speech by the desirability of the effects.

It should be apparent that there is risk involved in assuming a direct connection between historical events and specific speeches. The critic cannot be absolutely sure of such direct connections. Yet an important function of the criticism is to point out how speeches work and what happens historically as a result of them. To do this, the critic must employ the methods of the historian to determine, as accurately as possible, the connections between speeches and historical events. When he does this well, he makes a contribution to historiography as well as to rhetoric.

Until recently, the specific effects created by various rhetorical factors in a speech have been largely ignored. Critics have looked at the larger or more general effects, such as changes in public opinion, institutional reforms, and changed voting patterns, which may have resulted from a speech or series of speeches. Now, experimental techniques are being used to determine how people respond to specific aspects of the communication situation.

Numerous experimental studies have been made in recent decades, measuring listener response to specific rhetorical devices. It has been found that the techniques of the social scientist can be employed to measure scientifically audience response to such variables as the amount and types of evidence used, the level of language, authority symbols, strong and moderate emotional appeals, speaker appearance, etc. These findings have greatly increased knowledge of the way in which rhetorical techniques actually work, besides providing a more complete view of the specific effects of communication.

These developments have resulted from a movement of ever-increasing proportions devoted to the science of human behavior. This movement, begun by the social psychologists (behaviorists) and now including linguists, anthropologists, physicists, and engineers, has produced new tools and experimental forms for measuring attitudes, attitude changes, motivation, the transmission and receiving of language symbols, the storing and retrieving of information, the conditioning of mental responses, and so on. The aim of the behavioral scientists is to develop hypotheses about behavior that can be scientifically demonstrated, i.e., to formulate a science of human behavior. This, of course, includes communication behavior—the form of behavior most accessible to the scientist. Consequently, a growing body of scientific data exists about the effects of communication. Some of these data have been used to develop communication models based upon measurable communication effects. Many of these are useful to the critic as comparative forms to which he can fit a speech and observe its effects. In addition to models, several new theories of communication have been developed based upon scientific data. Some of the better-known ones are Leon Festinger's "cognitive dissonance" theory,[1] Shannon and Weaver's "mathematical or informational" theory,[2] and Norbert Wiener's "cybernetic" theory.[3] Each of these theories accounts for communication effects through scientific measurement rather than through empirical deduction. Each can be useful to the speech critic in meeting that difficult problem—assessing the actual effects of a speech.

Along with this scientific study of behavior has come the development of statistical procedures and computers that have greatly facilitated scientific measurement. It is now possible, for example, to calculate, in a matter of minutes, the statistical significance of the amount of opinion or attitude change in a group of auditors. It is also possible, through selective sampling and application of a statistical formula, to determine opinions of whole populations. All these techniques provide the critic with more objective means of determining the effects of communication.[4]

The employment of shift-of-opinion ballots, attitude scales, electronic devices to measure attention and nervous reactions, and indepth interviewing have provided an ever-increasing body of knowledge about the effects of communication, which the critic can use to ascertain the outcomes of a given speech. Much of this scientific measurement has corroborated past empirical conclusions, but some findings have forced us to discard notions about what happens when the speaker uses certain rhetorical techniques. For example, it has been established that very strong fear-arousing appeals usually lessen rather than heighten the impact of the speaker's message, because people would have to alter their patterns of thinking and conduct too drastically if they admitted to themselves that the situation was as fearful as the speaker claimed. Findings such as these

[1] Leon Festinger, **A Theory of Cognitive Dissonance** (Evanston: Northwestern University Press, 1957).
[2] Claude Shannon and Warren Weaver, **The Mathematical Theory of Communication** (Urbana: The University of Illinois Press, 1962).
[3] Norbert Wiener, **Cybernetics: or Control and Communication in the Animal and Machine** (New York: Wiley, 1948).
[4] For an extensive survey of experimental research and findings in speech, the reader is referred to Ernest G. Bormann, **Theory and Research in the Communicative Arts** (New York: Holt, Rinehart and Winston, 1965).

are invaluable to the critic in pinpointing the effects of a speech, and they add greatly to the store of rhetorical knowledge he uses in making his evaluations.

There is no doubt about the value of scientific measurement of communication effects. However, these measurements **do not substitute** for the critical function of evaluation and judgment. Experimental research can help in correlating rhetorical technique with audience response, in testing rhetorical methods, in determining how language functions, and in broadening and strengthening rhetorical theory; but by its very nature scientific measurement cannot produce judgments or evaluations. This can be done only by a critic, who, through his knowledge of rhetoric, understanding of speech practices, and awareness of communication measurements, has formed a standard of effectiveness that he can apply in making subjective judgments. This point has been well summed up in an article by Albert J. Croft:

> ... The critic must be willing to immerse himself in the available data on the speech in its time, and then to make a straightforward judgment on the manner in which the speaker used the "best available means of persuasion" in terms of the specific ideas of the speaker and his audience. Such judgments will involve personal estimates of the objective "rightness" of the speaker's systems of values, as well as of the potential effectiveness of these values as persuasion. No experimental or scientific device can be substituted for these processes, nor should it be. This situation is not an evil; on the contrary, it may yet force us to produce the greatest contribution which criticism can make.[5]

The critic is placed in a dilemma because speech is a response-getting activity and should, therefore, be evaluated by **its effect.** How, then, is a critic to evaluate a speech that is not for an immediate audience, and does not seek specific results, such as Sir Thomas More's speech on the scaffold? What of a speech that is written but never delivered, such as Milton's **Areopagitica,** or any other speech that is not intended for a specific audience or does not seek an immediate response? Admittedly, this type of speech is rare. However, the critic does encounter speeches that do not fit the usual persuasive-informative categories.

[5] Albert J. Croft, "The Functions of Rhetorical Criticism," **The Quarterly Journal of Speech,** XLII (October 1956), 290.

The quality of the speech

Evaluating a speech by effects alone can make it difficult for the critic to justify his evaluation of the usual, as well as unusual, speech. He may find it impossible to determine the exact effects of a speech; there may be literally no end to such effects. The critic could find himself in the position of chasing after effects so exclusively that he neglects the speech itself.

Those speeches most often praised are frequently the most difficult to assess in terms of actual effects. Witness Demosthenes' speeches on the threat of the Macedonians, Edmund Burke's speeches in opposition to the war on the American colonies, Lincoln's Gettysburg Address, and Woodrow Wilson's speeches in favor of joining the League of Nations. These speeches would have to be judged failures if a critic applied only the "results" standard. Even if a critic sought the cumulative effects rather than immediate results, he would be hard pressed to establish exactly what these effects were. Rather, each of these speeches has a quality that makes it significant as a rhetorical effort.

The study of the quality of speeches provides critics with a method of evaluating speeches apart from specific results. In this method, the critic assesses the **artistic quality** of the speech as a literary genre. The critic looks at effects, not for effects' sake, but to help him in judging the quality of the speech.

Why does the critic look at the quality rather than the effects of a speech, aside from the difficulties of determining effects? Because rhetoric is a **faculty** for discovering the means of persuasion. It is not a technique or set of rules for the speaker in a particular context—the speaker must **create** his own persuasive forms adapted to his particular situation. How creatively or artistically he does this determines the quality of the work. The painter may be taught the principles of color and line and design, but he must put this knowledge to work in a way that will create a unique painting. It is this quality of uniqueness that the art critic looks for in judging the painting. The same thing is done by the speech critic; he looks for the artistic quality of each discourse, compared to what might have been said, what the situation called for, and what resources were available.

How does the critic evaluate the quality of a speech? He looks for the same things the literary critic or art critic does: truth, beauty, universality, force, and design. He looks for these qualities in the **language and form** of the speech, though he may use certain extrinsic factors to help him reveal them. He wants to know if the speaker has said something that furthers truth or helps man to cope with reality. We know that life is divisive, disruptive, ever-changing, and that enumeration of facts or statements that seek mere discursive understanding are not adequate to sharpen and expand man's vision so that he can see through the confusion to the more permanent or universal truths. Each speaker asks listeners to respond to his presentation of reality. He has at his disposal logic, forms of argument, modes of proof, and language structures that can be blended creatively to inspire his listeners in the quest for wisdom, good laws, justice, and individual betterment. The critic has both historical and contemporary speech models that demonstrate the high quality with which some men have used rhetorical forms to energize truth.

Speeches not only bring man closer to truth, they also inspire through their aesthetic qualities. Rationality is indispensable to speech, but so is emotional inspiration. Men have the capacity to feel and suffer, to know pleasure, as well as to think. This capacity, through the artistic use of language, can be utilized to arouse and move men. Language rhythms and sounds, and such language forms as figures and metaphors, can be employed to give speeches an aesthetic beauty that provides pleasure and inspiration for the listener. Just as an architectural structure can have a quality of beauty as well as a functional use, a speech can be beautiful as well as truthful. The speaker can, for example, use alliteration and balanced sentences that will heighten the impact of his ideas through the auditory pleasure and appreciation of poetic beauty that they create. By the same token, a speech that is sound in thought and argument can be jarring and distracting to the listener because of the discord created by ill-chosen words and poorly structured sentences. Nevertheless, in evaluating the beauty of a speech, the critic should keep in mind that stylistic devices can be overdone, to the point where the listener is so involved in the aesthetic experience that he loses sight of the ideas being conveyed.

To judge the quality of the speech, the critic considers also the universality of the speaker's appeals. Almost all speakers make use of emotional appeals; they appeal to the imaginative side of man to stimulate thought and move him to action. These appeals can also be to the more base and unenlightened desires of men, as is obvious from the suspicion directed toward any emotional appeal in speech-making. On the other hand, those discourses that are the most highly regarded all contain strong emotional appeals that move men to seek unselfish aims, to serve others in good causes, and to be more ethical in thought and action. The critic, in evaluating the universal qualities of the speech, looks for the speaker's use of those appeals that urge men to seek truth and better understanding of themselves and the social consequences of their actions. The critic watches for the employment of those appeals that are universal in the sense that they represent the highest aims of our society. He will eschew the appeal of quick and easy answers to complex problems, and he will judge highly those speeches that provide men with thoughts and points of view to which they can return again to find direction and comfort.

In evaluating force and design, or form, the critic appraises the means, both auditory and visual, used by the speaker to make his listeners attentive to his ideas and aware of his contributions. The critic will examine the way in which the speaker has developed and ordered his thoughts and structured his language, in order to determine any uniqueness in statement and organization that would make the listener or reader want to "reach out" for the meaning and import of the speaker's ideas. Some statements have force because they are a particularly apt analysis of an underlying problem or feeling. Such is Franklin D. Roosevelt's statement "We have nothing to fear but fear itself," in his first inaugural address. Other statements are forceful because they bring together a whole range of beliefs, attitudes, and hopes, as does Lincoln's "that government of the people, by the people, and for the people, shall not perish from the earth." Some speeches are unique in design, impelling listeners to keep listening because of the interesting way in which ideas are being related. Other speeches are notable because the speaker puts together that which has been scattered and incomprehensible into a form that clarifies and unifies the thinking of the auditors.

An excellent example of this kind of evaluation can be seen in this excerpt from Chauncey Goodrich's criticism of the speaking of

William Pitt the Elder, Lord Chatham, "the Great Commoner" of the British Parliament in the latter part of the eighteenth century.

> ... The leading characteristic of eloquence is **force;** and force in the orator depends mainly on the action of strongly-excited feeling on a powerful intellect. The intellect of Chatham was of the highest order, and was peculiarly fitted for the broad and rapid combinations of oratory. It was at once comprehensive, acute, and vigorous; enabling him to embrace the largest range of thought; to see at a glance what most men labor out by slow degrees; and to grasp his subject with a vigor, and hold on to it with a firmness, which have rarely, if ever, been equaled. But his intellect never acted alone. It was impossible for him to speak on any subject in a dry or abstract manner; all the operations of his mind were pervaded and governed by intense feeling. This gave rise to certain characteristics of his eloquence which may here be mentioned.
>
> First, he did not, like many in modern times, divide a speech into distinct compartments, one designed to convince the understanding, and another to move the passions and the will. They were too closely united in his own mind to allow of such a separation. All went together, conviction and persuasion, intellect and feeling, like chain-shot.
>
> Secondly, the rapidity and abruptness with which he often flashed his thoughts upon the mind arose from the same source. Deep emotion strikes directly at its object. It struggles to get free from all secondary ideas—all mere accessories. Hence the simplicity, and even bareness of thought, which we usually find in the great passages of Chatham and Demosthenes. The whole turns often on a single phrase, a word, an allusion. They put forward a few great objects, sharply defined, and standing boldly out in the glowing atmosphere of emotion. They pour their burning thoughts instantaneously upon the mind, as a person might catch the rays of the sun in a concave mirror, and turn them on their object with a sudden and consuming power.
>
> Thirdly, his mode of reasoning, or, rather, of dispensing with the forms of argument, resulted from the same cause. It is not the fact, though sometimes said, that Lord Chatham never reasoned. In most of his early speeches, and in some of his later ones, especially those on the right of taxing America, we find many examples of argument; brief, indeed, but remarkably clear and stringent. It is true, however, that he endeavored, as far as possible, to escape from the trammels of formal reasoning. When the mind is all aglow with a subject, and

sees its conclusion with the vividness and certainty of intuitive truths, it is impatient of the slow process of logical deduction. It seeks rather to reach the point by a bold and rapid progress, throwing away the intermediate steps, and putting the subject **at once** under such aspects and relations as to carry its own evidence along with it. Demosthenes was remarkable for thus crushing together proof and statement in a single mass. When, for example, he calls on his judges . . . not to make his enemy their counselor as to the manner in which they should hear his reply, there is an argument involved in the very ideas brought together—in the juxtaposition of the words . . . an argument the more forcible because not drawn out in a regular form. It was so with Lord Chatham. The strength of his feelings bore him directly forward to the **results** of argument. He affirmed them earnestly, positively, not as mere assertions, but on the ground of their intrinsic evidence and certainty. John Foster has finely remarked, that "Lord Chatham struck on the results of reasoning as a cannon-shot strikes the mark, without your seeing its course through the air." Perhaps a **bombshell** would have furnished even a better illustration. It explodes when it strikes, and thus becomes the most powerful of **arguments.**

Fourthly, this ardor of feeling, in connection with his keen penetration of mind, made him often indulge in political prophecy. His predictions were, in many instances, surprisingly verified. We have already seen it in the case of Admiral Hawke's victory, and in his quick foresight of a war with Spain in 1762. . . . As he advanced in years, his tone of admonition, especially on American affairs, became more and more lofty and oracular. He spoke as no other man ever spoke in a great deliberative assembly—as one who felt that the time of his departure was at hand; who, withdrawn from the ordinary concerns of life, in the words of his great eulogist, "came **occasionally** into our system to **counsel and decide."**

Fifthly, his great preponderance of feeling made him, in the strictest sense of the term, an extemporaneous speaker. His mind was, indeed, richly furnished with thought upon every subject which came up for debate, and the matter he brought forward was always thoroughly matured and strikingly appropriate; but he seems never to have studied its arrangement, much less to have bestowed any care on the language, imagery, or illustrations. Everything fell into its place at the moment. He poured out his thoughts and feelings just as they arose in his mind; and hence, on one occasion, when dispatches had been received which could not safely be made public, he said to one of his colleagues, "I must not speak today; I shall let out the secret." It is also worthy of remark, that nearly all these great passages, which came with such startling power upon the House, arose out of some unexpected turn of the debate, some incident or expression which called forth, at the moment, these sudden bursts of eloquence. . . .

To this intense emotion, thus actuating all his powers, Lord Chatham united a vigorous and lofty imagination, which formed his crowning excellence as an orator. It is this faculty which exalts **force** into the truest and most sublime eloquence. In this respect he approached more nearly than any speaker of modern times, to the great master of Athenian art. . . . The imagination of Lord Chatham struck directly at its object. It "flew an eagle flight, forth and right on." It never became his master. Nor do we ever find it degenerating into **fancy**, in the limited sense of that term: it was never **fanciful**. It was, in fact, so perfectly blended with the other powers of his mind—so simple, so true to nature even in its loftiest flights—that we rarely think of it as imagination at all.

. . . The words are admirably chosen. The sentences are not rounded or balanced periods, but are made up of short clauses which flash themselves upon the mind with all the vividness of distinct ideas, and yet are closely connected together as tending to the same point, and uniting to form larger masses of thought. Nothing can be more easy, varied, and natural than the style of these speeches. There is no mannerism about them. They contain some of the most vehement passages in English oratory; and yet there is no appearance of effort, no straining after effect. They have this infallible mark of genius—they make every one feel, that if placed in like circumstances, he would have said exactly the same things in the same manner. "Upon the whole," in the words of Mr. Grattan, "there was in this man something that could create, subvert, or reform; an understanding, a spirit, and an eloquence to summon mankind to society, or to break the bonds of slavery asunder, and rule the wildness of free minds with unbounded authority; something that could establish or overwhelm empire, and strike a blow in the world that should resound through its history."[6]

It should be noted that the critic assessing the quality of a speech can never divorce it completely from its audience and occasion. The artistic excellence of a speech will always have to be evaluated in terms of the way in which it is designed to influence people. Unlike poetical discourse, which gives expression to the imagination of the

[6]Chauncey A. Goodrich, **Selected British Eloquence** (Indianapolis: Bobbs-Merrill, 1963), pp. 73–75. Reprinted by permission of the publisher.

writer, rhetorical discourse exists to channel the understanding and attitude of audiences. As Wichelns put it: ". . . the writer of rhetorical discourse is, in a sense, perpetually in bondage to the occasion and the audience; and in that fact we find the line of cleavage between rhetoric and poetic."[7]

The artistic quality of a speech is assessed by means of comparisons with the artistic excellence of other speakers and writers. The critic determines what would constitute the most artistically excellent use of the available means of persuasion. Knowing what can be expected of a speaker because he has learned what has been judged as high quality in other discourses, he can have at hand a touchstone of judgment. However, he must avoid the error of making all speeches conform to some ancient standard that is no longer applicable. Though most values and virtues in Western civilization have changed very little, circumstances do change, and with them the needs of men and the language used to express those needs. We still seek honorable actions in the conduct of political affairs, justice in the settlement of disputes, and dignity in the pursuit of happiness, just as did the ancient Athenians. However, in our times new demands are made on speakers—to reach ever-larger audiences, to produce solutions of greater complexity, and to utilize the language structures of the masses. Thus, the critic must evaluate the quality of a speech against the backdrop of social circumstances—that is, he must assess its worth to the society in which it exists, as well as judge its artistic quality.

The worth of the speech

The most difficult critical judgment for the critic is that of the ultimate worth of the object he is criticizing. It is difficult because it is the most speculative judgment he is called upon to produce. It requires a wide knowledge of the society in which the critic operates. It entails interpretations of systems of values—those of the speaker, the audience, and the critic.

Evaluating the worth of a speech involves an assessment of the social consequences of the speech. This is similar to, but not exactly the same as, evaluating the rhetorical effects of a speech. In examining

[7]Herbert Wichelns, "The Literary Criticism of Oratory," in **The Rhetorical Idiom**, ed. Donald C. Bryant (Ithaca: Cornell University Press, 1958), p. 38.

the worth of the speech, the critic looks at the larger social purposes and the ultimate ends or values of society, and he fits the speech into the stream of social thought and action in order to determine its contribution to the goals of society.

From ancient times to the present, rhetorical discourses have been recognized as both reflecters and formulaters of public morality. Plato sought forms of discourse that could provide men with the knowledge of the Idea of the Good. Aristotle provided a philosophy and method of discourse that would allow men to develop their logical and moral potential. The ancients conceived of speechmaking as the energizer of truth and a means to the perfectability of man and society. Isocrates, the Athenian orator-statesman-teacher, taught:

> ... generally speaking, there is no institution devised by man which the power of speech has not helped us to establish. For this it is which has laid down laws concerning things just and unjust, and things base and honorable; and if it were not for these ordinances we should not be able to live with one another. It is by this also that we confute the bad and extol the good. Through this we educate the ignorant and appraise the wise; for the power to speak well is taken as the surest index of a sound understanding, and discourse which is true and lawful and just is the outward image of a good and faithful soul. With this faculty we both contend against others on matters which are open to dispute and seek light for ourselves on things which are unknown; for the same arguments which we use in persuading others when we speak in public, we employ also when we deliberate in our own thoughts.[8]

Isocrates' statement foreshadowed that modern dictum: "We begin speaking as we think and we end thinking as we speak."

Modern rhetoricians and linguists are aware that the values and conduct of a society cannot be separated from the utterances of the people who make up that society. They help bring about a relationship between speeches and the acts or events, and these acts or events help formulate thought patterns and value systems of the society. No society can hold to beliefs that value the dignity and worth of the individual while it entertains and encourages utterances that debase human passions and degrade human activities.

[8] Isocrates, "Antidosis," **Isocrates**, trans. George Norlin (Cambrigde, Massachusetts: Harvard University Press [The Loeb Classical Library], 1928), pp. 79–81.

No society can remain democratic that allows and encourages discourses that call for means and ends that are basically undemocratic. Sooner or later, these statements and their ensuing actions reshape our thought patterns and value systems if they are allowed to go unchecked. At this point, the critic serves our greatest need. By judging the worth of rhetorical discourses, he reminds us of the larger social purposes and the ultimate values that society seeks to actualize.

The speech critic must finally place his judgment of a speech in the realm of values. No judgment of the effectiveness of a speaker or the artistic qualities of a speech can be complete without ethical and moral evaluation. Richard Weaver reminds us of this fact:

> No one can live a life of direction and purpose without some scheme of values. As rhetoric confronts us with choices involving values, the rhetorician is a preacher to us, noble if he tries to direct our passion toward noble ends and base if he uses our passion to confuse and degrade us. Since all utterance influences us in one or the other of these directions, it is important that the direction be the right one. . . ."[9]

The critic, by evaluating the worth of a speech, makes his contribution to our pursuit of noble ends.

To make a judgment of the worth of a speech the critic must know rhetorical theory, understand the qualities of rhetorical excellence, and be aware of the purposes of society and the values that it seeks. The aims and goals of our democracy have been frequently stated and widely discussed. We have a great heritage of literature expounding these aims, and an educational system that has as its foundation the training of citizens for active participation in a democratic society. The critic draws from these sources in formulating judgments about a speech's contribution to our democratic society. He can make his judgment by judicious application of past experiences and by careful consideration of possible consequences. Such a judgment should provide what is called socially responsible speech criticism.

Thomas R. Nilsen has suggested a plan for judging the contribution of a speech to the purpose of society. Judgments should be based on the extent to which the speech:

[9] Richard Weaver, "Language Is Sermonic," in **Dimensions of Rhetorical Scholarship,** ed. Roger Nebergall (Norman: University of Oklahoma Press, 1963) p. 63.

1. Is consistent within itself and with the observed events of the time;
2. Arouses in the minds of its hearers, and later readers, as accurate a concept of the events with which it deals as possible;
3. Places foremost the ultimate goals of society and relates its immediate purpose to these goals;
4. Examines explicitly, as far as reasonably possible, the social consequences, direct and indirect, of the actions it may urge.[10]

These judgments require the critic to go beyond the application of rhetorical values and to consider the larger social values that rhetoric is supposed to serve.

This final requirement of judging the social worth of a speech places a severe burden on the critic. It requires him to venture into the realms of philosophy, political science, sociology, and psychology. But then these are the areas which are affected by communication, and the speech critic cannot shirk the responsibility of pointing out the consequences of our utterances. To assume that speaking has no social consequences would relegate persuasive discourse to the category of parlor games. To assume that the consequences of persuasive discourse cannot be evaluated would make rhetoric capricious at best and a menace at worst.

Kenneth Burke, whose critical theories were discussed in Chapter 4, believes firmly that all utterances have social consequences, and he does not shirk the responsibility of evaluating the worth of a statement. Appraising Hitler's utterances in **Mein Kampf,** Burke makes the following judgments:

> What are we to learn from Hitler's book? For one thing, I believe that he has shown, to a very disturbing degree, the power of endless repetition. Every circular advertising a Nazi meeting had, at the bottom, two slogans: "Jews not admitted" and "War victims free." And the substance of Nazi propaganda was built about these two "complementary themes. . . .
>
> . . . is it possible that an equally important feature of appeal was not so much in the repetitiousness per se, but in the fact that, by means of it, Hitler provided a "world view" for people who had previously seen the world but piecemeal? Did not much of his lure derive, once more, from the **bad** filling of a **good** need? Are not those who insist upon a purely **planless** working of the market asking people to

[10]Thomas R. Nilsen, "Criticism and Social Consequences," **The Quarterly Journal of Speech,** XLII (April 1956), 177.

accept far too slovenly a scheme of human purpose, a slovenly scheme that can be accepted so long as it operates with a fair degree of satisfaction, but becomes abhorrent to the victims of its disarray? Are they not then psychologically ready for a rationale, any rationale, if it but offer them some specious "universal" explanation? Hence, I doubt whether the appeal was in the sloganizing element alone (particularly as even slogans can only be hammered home, in speech after speech, and two or three hours at a stretch, by endless variations on the themes). And Hitler himself somewhat justifies my interpretation by laying so much stress upon the **half-measures** of the middle-class politicians, and the contrasting **certainty** of his own methods. He was not offering people a **rival** world view; rather, he was offering a world view to people who had no other to pit against it.

As for the basic Nazi trick: the "curative" unification by a fictitious devil-function, gradually made convincing by the sloganizing repetitiousness of standard advertising technique—the opposition must be as unwearying in the attack upon it. It may well be that people, in their human frailty, require an enemy as well as a goal. Very well: Hitlerism itself has provided us with such an enemy—and the clear example of its operation is guaranty that we have, in him and all he stands for, no purely fictitious "devil-function" made to look like a world menace by rhetorical blandishments, but a reality whose ominousness is clarified by the record of its conduct to date. . . .

But above all, I believe, we must make it apparent that Hitler appeals by relying upon a bastardization of fundamentally religious patterns of thought. In this, if properly presented, there is no slight to religion. There is nothing in religion proper that requires a fascist state. There is much in religion, when misused, that does lead to a fascist state. There is a Latin proverb, **Corruptio optimi pessima,** "the corruption of the best is the worst." And it is the corruptors of religion who are a major menace to the world today, in giving the profound patterns of religious thought a crude and sinister distortion.

Our job, then, our anti-Hitler Battle, is to find all available ways of making the Hitlerite distortions of religion apparent, in order that politicians of his kind in America be unable to perform a similar swindle. The desire for unity is genuine and admirable. The desire for national unity, in the present state of the world, is genuine and admirable. But this unity, if attained on a deceptive basis, by emotional trickeries that shift our criticism from the accurate locus of our trouble, is no unity at all. For, even if we are among those who happen to be "Aryans," we solve no problems even for ourselves by such solutions, since the factors pressing towards calamity remain.

Thus, in Germany, after all the upheaval, we see nothing beyond a drive for ever more and more upheaval, precisely because the "new way of life" was no new way, but the dismally oldest way of sheer deception—hence, after all the "change," the factors driving towards unrest are left intact, and even strengthened. True, the Germans had the resentment of a lost war to increase their susceptibility to Hitler's rhetoric. But in wider sense, it has repeatedly been observed, the whole world lost the War—and the accumulating ills of the capitalist order were but accelerated in their movements towards confusion. Hence, here too there are the resentments that go with frustration of men's ability to work and earn. At that point a certain kind of industrial or financial monopolist may, annoyed by the contrary voices of our parliament, wish for the momentary peace of one voice, amplified by social organizations, with all the others not merely quieted, but given the quietus. So he might, under Nazi promptings, be tempted to back a group of gangsters who, on becoming the political rulers of the state, would protect him against the necessary demands of the workers. His gangsters, then, would be his insurance against his workers. But who would be his insurance against his gangsters?[11]

Epilogue

Every man in a free society is a rhetorical critic and a practitioner of the art of rhetoric. We all endeavor to exert influence through our statements, and we all pass judgments on speeches and writings that affect us. In a free society, this is both a privilege and a responsibility. We have the right to free inquiry, free expression, and free thought, but these rights in turn must serve the ends of a democratic society if it is to survive and we are to remain free. Consequently, all of us must be aware of the means and methods by which we secure these benefits and extend the goals of our free society. Quite obviously, the most important means of accomplishing these ends is through responsible, effective communication.

To make the best possible use of communication, we must become expert in the use of it, and we must continue the study of it scientifically and empirically. We need to learn all that is possible about the workings of words, the responses of human beings to symbols, and the effects of communication on society. The task of

[11] Kenneth Burke, **The Philosophy of Literary Form** (Baton Rouge: Louisiana State University Press, 1941), pp. 217–220. Reprinted by permission of the author.

the rhetorical critic is to contribute to the understanding of communication. Rhetorical criticism is an extension of the theory and practice of effective discourse. Its function is to examine and judge the performance of the art of rhetoric. Its purpose is to maintain standards of excellence for the betterment of the art. The rhetorical critic, through description, analysis, interpretation, and evaluation of particular communications, helps clarify rhetorical theory, establish the limits of our present theory, formulate criteria for judgment of performance, and assess the influence of rhetorical discourse on society. Criticism is a discipline and an art that can be learned and performed with a high degree of skill. To the person who undertakes mastery of the art of rhetorical criticism, it affords an opportunity to contribute to a most important aspect of our democratic society.

Selected bibliography

The nature of criticism

Atkins, J. W. H. **Literary Criticism in Antiquity.** London: Cambridge University Press, 1934.

Black, Edwin. **Rhetorical Criticism.** New York: Macmillan, 1965.

Burke, Kenneth. **The Philosophy of Literary Form.** Baton Rouge: Louisiana State University Press, 1941.

Crane, R. S., ed. **Critics and Criticism, Ancient and Modern.** Chicago: University of Chicago Press, 1952.

Frye, Northrop. **Anatomy of Criticism: Four Essays.** Princeton: Princeton University Press, 1957.

Greene, Theodore M. **The Arts and the Art of Criticism.** Princeton: Princeton University Press, 1940.

Kant, Immanuel. **Critique of Practical Reason,** trans. T. K. Abbott. 6th ed. London: Longmans, 1927.

Levin, Harry. **Contexts of Criticism.** Cambridge: Harvard University Press, 1957.

Nichols, Marie Hochmuth. **Rhetoric and Criticism.** Baton Rouge: Louisiana State University Press, 1963.

Richards, I. A. **Practical Criticism: A Study of Literary Judgment.** New York: Harcourt, Brace, 1929.

———. **Principles of Literary Criticism.** London: Routledge & Kegan Paul, 1924.

Spencer, Herbert. **The Philosophy of Style.** New York: Appleton, 1871.

Thonssen, Lester, and Baird, A. Craig. **Speech Criticism.** New York: Ronald, 1948.

The rationale of rhetoric

Adams, John Quincy. **Lectures on Rhetoric and Oratory,** 2 vols. New York and Cambridge: Hilliard and Metcalf, 1810.

Aristotle. **The "Rhetoric" and "Poetics,"** ed. Friedrich Solmsen. New York: Modern Library, 1954.

———. **The Rhetoric of Aristotle,** trans. Lane Cooper. New York: Appleton, 1932.

Baird, A. Craig. **Rhetoric: A Philosophical Inquiry.** New York: Ronald, 1965.

Baldwin, Charles Sears. **Ancient Rhetoric and Poetic.** New York: Macmillan, 1924.

———. **Medieval Rhetoric and Poetic.** New York: Macmillan, 1928.

Blair, Hugh. **Lectures on Rhetoric and Belles Lettres.** 8th ed. 3 vols. London: T. Cadell, Jun. and W. Davies in the Strand & W. Greech, Edinburgh, 1801; 6th ed. London: A. Strahan and T. Cadell, 1796.

Bormann, Ernest G. **Theory and Research in the Communicative Arts.** New York: Holt, Rinehart & Winston, 1965.

Bryant, Donald C. "Aspects of Rhetorical Tradition: The Intellectual Foundation," **The Quarterly Journal of Speech,** XXXVI (April 1950, October 1950).

———. "Rhetoric: Its Function and Scope," **The Quarterly Journal of Speech,** XXXIX (December 1953).

Burke, Kenneth. "Rhetoric—Old and New," **The Journal of General Education,** V (April 1951).

———. **A Grammar of Motives.** New York: Prentice-Hall, 1945.

———. **A Rhetoric of Motives.** New York: Prentice-Hall, 1950.

Campbell, George. **The Philosophy of Rhetoric,** ed. Lloyd F. Bitzer. Carbondale: Southern Illinois University Press, 1963.

Clark, Donald L. **Rhetoric in Greco-Roman Education.** New York: Columbia University Press, 1957.

Eubanks, Ralph T., and Baker, Virgil L. "Toward an Axiology of Rhetoric," **The Quarterly Journal of Speech,** XLVIII (1962).

Fogarty, Daniel. **Roots for a New Rhetoric.** New York: Teachers College, Columbia University Press, 1959.

Genung, John F. **The Practical Elements of Rhetoric.** Boston: Ginn, 1886.

Hunt, Everett, "Rhetoric as a Humane Study," **The Quarterly Journal of Speech,** XLI (April 1955).

Kennedy, George. **The Art of Persuasion in Greece.** Princeton: Princeton University Press, 1963.

McBurney, James H. "The Place of the Enthymeme in Rhetorical Theory," **Speech Monographs,** III (1936).

Natanson, Maurice. "The Limits of Rhetoric," **The Quarterly Journal of Speech,** XLI (April 1955).

Ong, Walter J., S.J. **Ramus: Method, and the Decay of Dialogue.** Cambridge: Harvard University Press, 1958.

Quintilian. **The Institutio Oratoria of Quintilian,** ... trans. H. E. Butler 4 vols. London: Heinemann; New York: G. P. Putnam, 1921.

Richards, I. A. **The Philosophy of Rhetoric.** New York: Oxford University Press, 1936; London: Kegan Paul and Trench, Trubner, 1929.

Shannon, Claude E., and Weaver, Warren. **The Mathematical Theory of Communication.** Urbana: The University of Illinois Press, 1949.

Wallace, Karl R. "The Substance of Rhetoric: Good Reasons," **The Quarterly Journal of Speech,** XLIX (October 1963).

Whately, Richard. **Elements of Rhetoric . . . ,** ed. Douglas Ehninger. Carbondale: Southern Illinois University Press, 1963.

The critical framework

Baird, A. Craig, and Thonssen, Lester. "Methodology in the Criticism of Public Address," **The Quarterly Journal of Speech,** XXXIII (April 1947).

Baskerville, Barnet. "Selected Writings on the Criticism of Public Address," **Western Speech Journal,** XXI (Spring 1957).

———. "Principal Themes of Nineteenth-Century Critics of Oratory," **Speech Monographs,** XIX (March 1952).

———. "Some American Critics of Public Address, 1850–1900," **Speech Monographs,** XVII (March 1950).

———. "The Dramatic Criticism of Oratory," **The Quarterly Journal of Speech,** XLV (February 1959).

Berlo, David K. **The Process of Communication.** New York: Holt, Rinehart & Winston, 1960.

Bryant, Donald C. "Some Problems of Scope and Method in Rhetorical Scholarship," **The Quarterly Journal of Speech,** XXIII (April 1937).

Burke, Kenneth. **Counter-Statement.** New York: Harcourt, Brace, 1931.

———. "A Dramatistic View of the Origins of Language," **The Quarterly Journal of Speech,** Part I, XXXVIII (October 1952); Part II, XXXVIII (December 1952); Part III, XXXIX (February 1953).

Cicero. **De Oratore,** in **Cicero on Oratory and Orators,** trans. J. S. Watson. New York: Harper, 1890.

Clark, Robert D. "Lesson from the Literary Critics," **Western Speech Journal,** XXI (Spring 1957).

Cohen, Herman. "Hugh Blair's Theory of Taste," **The Quarterly Journal of Speech,** XLIV (October 1958).

Croft, Albert J. "The Functions of Rhetorical Criticism," **The Quarterly Journal of Speech,** XLII (October 1956).

Dionysius of Halicarnassus. **On Literary Composition,** ed. W. Rhys Roberts. London: Macmillan, 1910.

Griffin, Leland M. "The Rhetoric of Historical Movements," **The Quarterly Journal of Speech,** XXXVIII (April 1952).

Grube, G. M. A. "Rhetoric and Literary Criticism," **The Quarterly Journal of Speech,** XLII (December 1956).

Haiman, Franklyn S. "Democratic Ethics and the Hidden Persuaders," **The Quarterly Journal of Speech,** XLIV (December 1958).

Hayakawa, S. I. **Language in Thought and Action.** 2nd ed. New York: Harcourt, Brace, 1964.

Hillbruner, Anthony. "Creativity and Contemporary Criticism," **Western Speech Journal,** XXIV (Winter 1960).

———. "Plato and Korzybski: Two Views of Truth and Rhetorical Theory," **The Southern Speech Journal,** XXIV (Summer 1959).

Holland, Laura V. "Kenneth Burke's Dramatistic Approach to Speech Criticism," **The Quarterly Journal of Speech,** XLI (December 1955).

———. "Rhetorical Criticism: A Burkeian Method," **The Quarterly Journal of Speech,** XXXIX (December 1953).

Hovland, Carl I., Janis, Irving L., and Kelley, Harold H. **Communication and Persuasion: Psychological Studies of Opinion Change.** New Haven: Yale University Press, 1953.

Hunt, Everett Lee. "Plato and Aristotle on Rhetoric and Rhetoricians," **Studies in Rhetoric and Public Speaking.** New York: Century, 1925.

———. "Rhetoric and Literary Criticism," **The Quarterly Journal of Speech,** XXI (November 1935).

Selected bibliography

Isocrates, trans. George Norlin. 3 vols. New York: The Loeb Classical Library, 1928.

Johnson, Allen. **The Historian and Historical Evidence.** New York: Scribner, 1926.

Johnson, Wendell. **People in Quandaries: The Semantics of Personal Adjustment.** New York: Harper, 1946.

Korzybski, Alfred. **Science and Sanity.** 3rd ed., rev. Lakeville, Conn.: The International Non-Aristotelian Library, 1948.

Lee, Irving J. "Four Ways of Looking at a Speech," **The Quarterly Journal of Speech,** XXVIII (April 1942).

Longinus, **De sublimitate** and Demetrius, **De elecutione.** London: The Loeb Classical Library, 1932.

Malony, Martin, J. "Some New Directions in Rhetorical Criticism," **Central States Speech Journal,** IV (1953).

Matthews, Jack. "A Behavioral Science Approach to the Study of Rhetoric," **The Pennsylvania Speech Annual,** XXI (1964).

McBurney, James H., and Wrage, Ernest J. **The Art of Good Speech.** Englewood Cliffs: Prentice-Hall, 1953.

Murphy, Richard. "The Speech as Literary Genre," **The Quarterly Journal of Speech,** XLIV (April 1958).

Murray, Elwood. "The Semantics of Rhetoric," **The Quarterly Journal of Speech,** XXX (February 1944).

Nilsen, Thomas R. "Criticism and Social Consequences," **The Quarterly Journal of Speech,** XLII (April 1956).

North, Helen F. "Rhetoric and Historiography," **The Quarterly Journal of Speech,** XLII (October 1956).

Ogden, C. K., and Richards, I. A. **The Meaning of Meaning.** London: Routledge & Kegan Paul, 1923.

Plato. . . . **Phaedrus, Ion, Gorgias, and Symposium,** . . . trans. Lane Cooper. London: Oxford University Press, 1938.

Priestley, Joseph. **A Course of Lectures on Oratory and Criticism,** eds. Vincent M. Bevilacqua and Richard Murphy. Carbondale: Southern Illinois University Press, 1965.

Redding, Charles. "Extrinsic and Intrinsic Criticism," **Western Speech Journal,** XXI (Spring 1957).

Reid, Loren P. "The Perils of Rhetorical Criticism," **The Quarterly Journal of Speech,** XXX (December 1944).

Richards, I. A. **Speculative Instruments.** Chicago: University of Chicago Press, 1955.

Thompson, Wayne N. "Contemporary Public Address: A Problem in Criticism," **The Quarterly Journal of Speech,** XL (February 1954).

Thonssen, Lester. "A Functional Interpretation of Aristotle's Rhetoric," **The Quarterly Journal of Speech,** XVI (June 1930).

Thucydides. **The Complete Writings of Thucydides,** trans. P. Crawley. New York: Random House, 1951.

Weaver, Richard M. **The Ethics of Rhetoric.** Chicago: Regnery, 1953.

Wiener, Norbert. **The Human Use of Human Beings: Cybernetics and Society.** Boston: Houghton Mifflin, 1954.

Wilson, John F., and Arnold, Carroll C. **Public Speaking as a Liberal Art.** Boston: Allyn and Bacon, 1964.

Wrage, Ernest J. "E. L. Godkin and the **Nation:** Critics of Public Address," **The Southern Speech Journal,** XV (December 1949).

–––. "Public Address: A Study in Social and Intellectual History," **The Quarterly Journal of Speech,** XXXIII (December 1947).

Speeches and criticisms

Auer, J. Jeffery. "Tom Corwin: 'King of the Stump,' " **The Quarterly Journal of Speech,** XXX (February 1944).

–––, ed. **Antislavery and Disunion, 1858–1861: Studies in the Rhetoric of Compromise and Conflict.** New York and Evanston: Harper & Row, 1963.

Baird, A. Craig, ed. **American Public Addresses, 1740–1952.** New York: McGraw-Hill, 1956.

Baskerville, Barnet. "Joe McCarthy, Brief Case Demagogue," **Today's Speech,** II (September 1954).

Behl, William A. "Theodore Roosevelt's Principles of Speech Preparation and Delivery," **Speech Monographs,** XII (1945).

Bormann, Ernest G. "A Rhetorical Analysis of the National Radio Broadcasts of Senator Huey Pierce Long," **Speech Monographs,** XXIV (November 1957).

Braden, Waldo W. "William E. Borah's Senate Speeches on the League of Nations, 1918–1920," **Speech Monographs,** X (1943).

–––, and Brandenburg, Earnest. "Roosevelt's Fireside Chats," **Speech Monographs,** XXII (November 1955).

Brandenburg, Earnest. "Franklin D. Roosevelt's International Speeches: 1939–1941," **Speech Monographs,** XVI (August 1949).

–––. "The Preparation of Franklin D. Roosevelt's Speeches," **The Quarterly Journal of Speech,** XXXV (April 1949).

Brigance, William N. **A History and Criticism of American Public Address.** 2 vols. New York: McGraw-Hill, 1943.

Crowell, Laura. "Franklin D. Roosevelt's Audience Persuasion in the 1936 Campaign," **Speech Monographs,** XVII (March 1950).

Eubank, Wayne C. "Benjamin Morgan Palmer's Lottery Speech, New Orleans, 1891," **The Southern Speech Journal,** XXIV (Fall 1958).

Goodrich, Chauncey A. **Select British Eloquence.** Indianapolis: Bobbs-Merrill, 1963.

Grover, David H. **Debaters and Dynamiters.** Corvallis: Oregon State University Press, 1964.

Haberman, Frederick W. "General MacArthur's Speech: A Symposium of Critical Comment," **The Quarterly Journal of Speech,** XXXVII (October 1951).

Hayes, Merwyn A. "William L. Yancey Presents the Southern Case to the North; 1860," **The Southern Speech Journal,** XXIX (Spring 1964).

Henderlider, Clair R. "Woodrow Wilson's Speeches on the League of Nations, September 4-25, 1919," **Speech Monographs,** XIII, (1946).

Hochmuth, Marie. **A History and Criticism of American Public Address.** Vol. III. New York: Longmans, 1955.

Hunter, Charles F. "Thomas Hart Benton: An Evaluation," **The Quarterly Journal of Speech,** XXX (October 1944).

Jebb, R. C., ed. **Attic Orators.** 2 vols. London: Macmillan, 1893.

Oliver, Robert T. "Wilson's Rapport with His Audience," **The Quarterly Journal of Speech,** XXVII (February 1941).

Parrington, Vernon L. **Main Currents of American Thought.** 3 vols. New York: Harcourt, Brace, 1921-1930.

Parrish, Wayland Maxwell, and Hochmuth, Marie, eds. **American Speeches.** New York: Longmans, 1954.

Perkins, Lindsey S. "The Oratory of Benjamin Ryan Tillman," **Speech Monographs,** XV (1948).

Streeter, Donald C. "The Major Public Addresses of Lucius Q. C. Lamar During the Period 1874 to 1890," **Speech Monographs,** XVI (August 1949).

Stelzner, Herman. "The British Orators, VII; John Morley's Speechmaking," **The Quarterly Journal of Speech,** XLV (April 1959).

Vasilew, Eugene. "Norman Thomas at the Townsend Convention of 1936," **Speech Monographs,** XXIV (November 1957).

Wallace, Karl R. "On the Criticism of the MacArthur Speech," **The Quarterly Journal of Speech,** XXXIX (February 1953).
Williams, Donald E. "Andrew D. White: Spokesman for the Free University," **The Quarterly Journal of Speech,** XLVII (April 1961).
Windes, Russel, Jr. "A Study in Effective and Ineffective Presidential Campaign Speaking," **Speech Monographs,** XXVIII (March 1961).
———, and Robinson, James A. "Public Address in the Career of Adlai E. Stevenson," **The Quarterly Journal of Speech,** XLII (October 1956).
Woodburn, James Albert, ed. **American Orations: Studies in American Political History.** 4 vols. New York and London: G. P. Putnam's Sons, The Knickerbocker Press, 1886.
Wylie, Philip. "Medievalism and the MacArthurian Legend," **The Quarterly Journal of Speech,** XXXVII (December 1951).

Collected essays on rhetoric and criticism

Bosmajian, Haig A., ed. **Readings in Speech.** New York: Harper & Row, 1965.
Bryant, Donald C., ed. **The Rhetorical Idiom.** Ithaca: Cornell University Press, 1958.
Bryson, Lyman, ed. **The Communication of Ideas.** New York: Harper, 1948.
Dexter, Lewis Anthony, and White, David Manning, eds. **People, Society, and Mass Communication.** New York: Free Press, 1964.
Howes, Raymond F., ed. **Historical Studies of Rhetoric and Rhetoricians.** Ithaca: Cornell University Press, 1961.
Murphy, Richard, ed. **Studies in Speech and Drama in Honor of Alexander M. Drummond.** Ithaca: Cornell University Press, 1944.
Nebergall, Roger E., ed. **Dimensions of Rhetorical Scholarship.** Norman: University of Oklahoma Press, 1963.
Schramm, Wilbur Lang, ed., **Communication in Modern Society.** Urbana: University of Illinois Press, 1948.
Schwartz, Joseph, and Rycenga, John A., eds. **The Province of Rhetoric.** New York: Ronald, 1965.
Wrage, Ernest J., and Baskerville, Barnet, eds. **American Forum: Speeches on Historic Issues, 1788–1900.** New York: Harper, 1960.

Index

Adaptation to audience, 63–64
A Grammar of Motives, 79ff
American Forum, 65
Analysis, 26–28
Analytic criticism, 17
Approaches to criticism, 18–19
Appropriateness, 11
  of choice, 37
A Rhetoric of Motives, 41
Areopagitica, 98
Argumentative discourse, 77–78
  (See also Genre of Argumentation)
Argumentative synthesis, 78
Aristotle, 4, 18, 45, 73
Arnold, Carroll C., 6, 20, 66, 68
Art of Good Speech, The, 20
Artistic qualities of speech, 99–101
Artistic standard, the, 20, 24–26
Attitude and Attitude Change, 64

Audience, the, 63–69
  resources within, 64
  responses, 40
Audience-speaker
  confrontation, 66
  interaction, 65
Auer, J. Jeffery, 56, 58
Baird, A. Craig, 13
Baskerville, Barnet, 65
Bass, Bernard M., 64
Bauer, Marvin G., 71, 73
Bauer, Raymond A., 66
Benton, Thomas Hart, speech-making interpreted, 62–63
Berlo, David K., 41
Beveridge, Albert J., speech on the disposition of the Philippine Islands analyzed, 50-51
Black, Edwin, 3, 18, 19, 74
Bormann, Ernest G., 68, 69, 97

Brigance, W. N., 51, 54, 73
Brown, J. A. C., 61
Bryant, Donald C., 2, 16
Bryson, Lyman, 64
Burke, Kenneth, 41, 79ff, 108
Canons of rhetoric, 18, 73
Chapman, John Jay, "Coatesville Address" analyzed, 76–77
Choice, factor of, 8
Cicero, 4
Cognitive dissonance, 97
Communication
  defined, 1
  judging the effect of, 1
  models, 96-97
Communication and Persuasion, 61
Communication of Ideas, The, 64
Corwin, Tom, speechmaking analyzed, 56–58
Critic, the, 2
  assuming the burden of proof, 30
Critical appraisal, 2
Critical judgment, 18, 89
Critical points of view, 15–20
  (**See also** types of criticism)
Criticism
  analytic, 17
  and learning, 11-12
  defined, 3
  impressionistic, 17
  judicial, 17
  making a case for, 30
  objectivity in, 2, 69, 73
  73

Criticism (cont.)
  rhetorical, 3
    (**See also** rhetorical criticism and speech critcism)
  social consequences of, 107-108
  types of, 15-20
Croft, Albert, 98
Curtis, George William, speechmaking interpreted, 66–68
Cybernetics, 97
Delivery, 19, 58–59
Description, 26–27
De Oratore, 4
Dimensions of Rhetorical Scholarship, 41, 107
Dramatistic criticism, 79–83
Effects of the speech, 93–98
Emotional proof, 51–52, 58
  (**See also** pathos)
Enthymeme, 46, 65–66
Ethical proof, 48–51, 58
  (**See also** ethos)
Ethical standard, the, 20, 23–24
Ethos, 45, 46, 48–51, 54
  (**See also** ethical proof)
Eubank, Wayne C., 65, 66
Evaluation, 26, 29–30
Exhortative-argumentative criticism, 74-79
Exhortative discourse, 75
Festinger, Leon, 97
General ends of speech, 40
General Semantics Movement, 85
Genre of argumentation, 72–79
  (**See also** argumentative discourse)

Index

Goodrich, Chauncey, 102, 104
Grady, Henry, the "New South" speech interpreted, 71–73
Haberman, Frederick, 70
Hayakawa, S. I., 86
Hayes, Merwyn A., 48, 49
Historical milieu, 70
History and Criticism of American Public Address, Vol. I, 54, 73; Vol. II, 51; Vol. III, 68
Hitler, Adolf, **Mein Kampf** criticized, 82–83, 108–110
Hochmuth, Marie, 68
Hovland, Carl I., 61
Howell, Wilbur, 53, 54
Hudson, Hoyt, 53, 54
Hunter, Charles F., 62, 63
Ideal performance, 25
Identification, 81–82
Impressionistic criticism, 17
Institutio Oratoria, 4, 24
Interpretation, 26–28
  and meaning, 60-61
  defined, 60
Invention, 18, 42–43, 80
Investigating the speech, 32–36
Isocrates, 106
Johnson, Wendell, 87
Judgment, 17, 89
Judicial criticism, 17
Judicious evaluation, 90–91
Korzybski, Alfred, 85ff
Lamar, Lucius Q.C., major public addresses, 1874–1890, analyzed, 47–48
Language, 54–55
  and emotion, 75-76
  and form, 100
  concrete, 75
  exhortative, 75
  forms, 86
  functions, 80 ,83-85
Language Habits in Human Affairs, 86
Language in Thought and Action, 86
Language-reality criticism, 85–88
Leadership, Psychology, and Organizational Behavior, 64
Lee, Irving J., 86, 87
Lincoln, Abraham, Second Inaugural Address criticized, 78–79
Lines of argument, 42–45
Logical argument, 46
  (**See also** logos)
Logos, 45, 46–48
  (**See also** logical argument)
Long, Huey Pierce, National Radio Broadcasts interpreted, 68–69
Longinus on the Sublime, 84
Lord Chatham, speechmaking evaluated, 102–104
Mathematical Theory of Communication, The, 97
McBurney, James H., 20
Meaning, 28, 60–61
Meaning of Meaning, 85
Mein Kampf, 82, 108
Methods of judgment, 91–92
Modes of proof, 45–46
Morley, John, speechmaking analyzed, 55–56

Movement study, 18
Nebergall, Roger E., 41
Neo-Aristotelian study, 18–19, 73
Nichols, Marie Hochmuth, 81
Nilsen, Thomas R., 107, 108
Non-Aristotelian interpretations, 73–88
Non-el principle, 86
Occasion, the, 69–73
 appropriateness for, 70-71
Old rhetoric, 81, 83
Organization, 52–53
 and arrangement, 18, 80
Palmer, Benjamin Morgan, lottery speech analyzed, 43–44
Pathos, 45, 46, 51–52, 54
 (**See also** emotional proof)
Pentad, Burke's, 80
People in Quandaries, 87
People, Society, and Mass Communication, 66
Phaedo, 23
Philosophy of Literary Form, The, 81ff, 110
Philosophy of Rhetoric, The 60, 83ff
Plato, 22
Practical Criticism, 85
Process of Communication, The, 41
Psychological interpretations, 62
Psychological study, 18
Public Speaking as a Liberal Art, 6, 20
Purpose, 9–11, 37

Purpose (cont.)
 of speech criticism, 6-11
Qualities of style, 54–55
Quality of a speech, 99–105
Quintilian, 4, 24
Rationale for speech criticism, 7–11
Response
 analysis of, 7
 of audience, 40
Results standard, the 20–22
Rhetoric, The 4, 18, 45, 73
Rhetoric and Criticism, 81
Rhetorical Criticism, 3, 18, 19, 74ff
Rhetorical Idiom, The, 16, 105
Rhetorical problem, the, 36–39
Rhetorical theory, 4, 8
Rhetorical transactions, 74–75
Richards, I. A., 60, 83ff
Ross, Herold Truslow, 50, 51
Science and Sanity, 86
Scientific measurement of speech, 96–98
Select British Eloquence, 104
Semantic reactions, 85–86
Shannon, Claude, 97
Sherif, Carolyn, 64
Social consequences, 105–106
Society and social values, 106–107
Speaker, the, 61–63
Speaker's intent, 40–41
Speech
 art of discourse, 4
 as an object of criticism, 3
 as social control, 9-10

Index

Speech (cont.)
  effects, 6
  purpose, 5, 6, 39–41, 94
Speech Criticism, 13, 17
Standards of judgment, 91
Stelzner, Herman, 55, 56
Strategies, 81–82
Streeter, Donald C., 47, 48
Student, the, and criticism, 11–13
Style, 18, 54–58
  (See also language)
Synthetic criticism, 17
Techniques of Persuasion, 61
Textual authenticity, 34–36
Theory and Research in the Communicative Arts, 97
Theory of Cognitive Discourse, A, 97
Thomas, Norman, speech to the Townsend Convention, 1936, analyzed, 38–39, 51–52

Thonssen, Lester, 13
Traditional speeches, 70–71
Trained critic, the, 6
Truth Standard, 20, 22–23
Types of judgment, 90
Values, 107
Vasilew, Eugene, 38, 39, 51, 52
Wallace, Karl, 70
Weaver, Richard M., 41, 46, 107
Weaver, Warren, 97
Webster, Daniel, speech on "Adams and Jefferson" analyzed, 53–54
Weiner, Norbert, 97
Wichelns, Herbert, 16, 105
Wilson, John F., 6, 20
Worth of the speech, 105–110
Wrage, Ernest J., 12, 20, 65
Wylie, Philip, 70
Yancey, William L., speeches presenting the Southern case to the North, 1860, analyzed, 48–49